THE MANAGEMENT OF METAL INVENTORIES

CLAUDE McMILLAN
University of Colorado, Boulder, Colo.

JOHN D. DEMAREE
University of Colorado, Boulder, Colo.

STEEL SERVICE CENTER INSTITUTE
540 Terminal Tower
Cleveland, Ohio   44113

preface

Since 1961 initiative among the leadership of the Steel Service Center Institute has led to an increasing involvement of a number of members of the academic community in the problems of metal service center management.

In close cooperation with these university representatives, a specialized continuing-education program has been developed for executives of metal service centers. The authors of this text are two of the academicians who are part of this continuing industry-university partnership. They have participated as instructors, conducted research, and now have prepared this text. They have been primarily responsible for the inventory management portion of this specialized educational program.

Inventory in any industrial distributing organization, such as metal service centers, is by far the largest single item of investment. Metal inventories in stock in North American service centers total in excess of one-billion dollars. The management of these inventories is therefore of primary importance and concern. Improved techniques in the management of inventories can make a major contribution to the betterment of service center earnings and customer service.

This text might be considered an interim report; an exposition of ideas and methods of applied value which have been distilled from the authors' association with men in the industry concerned with operating problems in the management of metal inventories. It is an interim report in the sense that the passage of time will require its revision. Their effort has been to mold theory into methods and procedures for applied analysis in the management of inventories.

Inventory managers in the metals industry operate in a dynamic environment, and the tools they bring to bear on problems will require modification if they are to be useful tomorrow. It is our hope, as well as the authors', that those who read and study this text, acting in the spirit of the industry-university partnership which yielded it, will feel a measure of responsibility for helping the authors make the modifications in future revisions required to maintain and improve its usefulness in the years ahead.

Robert G. Welch, President
Steel Service Center Institute

acknowledgment

Identifying all those whose influence is manifest in this volume would be impracticable. It includes, in addition to the President of the Steel Service Center Institute and his staff, a considerable portion of the executives and operating managers of the industry who have shared with the authors their knowledge, experience and judgment over the past four years. Their help and collaboration are deeply appreciated.

The years since 1961, when the authors first started participating in the industry-university partnership with the Steel Service Center Institute and its members, have been years of educational enrichment for us as we became more intimately conversant with the challenging problems of effective service center management.

A special word of appreciation is extended to Dr. Martin Basic whose studies of the gamma distribution are responsible for a significant portion of the text.

Claude McMillan
John D. Demaree

table of contents

SYMBOL GLOSSARY

DPY = Demand Per Year
LT = Lead Time
CPU = Cost Per Unit
COP = Cost Of Possession
AHC = Annual Holding Cost
AOC = Annual Ordering Cost
ASC = Annual Stockout Cost
AMC = Annual Materials Cost
R = Reorder Point
Q = Order Quantity
DDLT = Demand During Lead Time
TAC = Total Annual Cost
EOQ = Economic Order Quantity
P (DDLT>R) = Probability that Demand During
      Lead Time will exceed the Reorder Point
E (DDLT>R) = Expected Stockout During Lead Time
TACIM = Total Annual Cost Including Materials

1 introduction

IN RECENT YEARS INVENTORY MANAGEMENT has become a topic of increasingly widespread interest, as evidenced by the large number of magazine articles and textbooks dealing with inventory management and control and the increasing number of computerized inventory control systems. The metals service center industry has shared in the renewed attention given to inventory management and control through its advertising program dealing with the "cost of possession" and inventory holding costs. In fact, the term "professional inventory managers" has been used in reference to metals service center executives. This description is indicative of the central importance of inventory management in the industry; in addition, the adjective "professional" implies the existence or practice of a body of principles, special knowledge, etc.

A recent study of inventory management practices in the metals service center industry has revealed a wide diversity of inventory management practices. While some of this diversity may be explained by the differences in size of firms, types of metals carried, etc., many of the differences in practice must be attributed to different conceptions of the best means for the management of multi-item inventories. The purpose of this text is to explain inventory theory and to illustrate some of the techniques for implementing this theory in the metals service center industry.

This introductory chapter is intended to provide a framework for the remaining material in the text. The importance of inventory management in the metals service center industry, a brief summary of current inventory management practices in the industry, the historical development of inventory theory, and the manner in which the computer is becoming an increasingly significant factor will be discussed. The final part of the introductory chapter describes the organization of the remainder of the text.

importance of inventory management in the industry

One means of discussing the importance of inventory management in the metals service center industry is through a brief review of the task of inventory management. A typical metals service center has thousands of items in stock, representing the largest portion of invested capitol in the business. In addition to the important task of inventory record-keeping, the recurrent questions for each stock-keeping unit are: *When* to replenish supply? In what *quantity* to replenish supply? The answers to these questions involve the interrelationships among a large number of variables. For example, basic material costs, rates of demand, quantity-extras schedules, lead times, number of customers, profit margins, etc., are among the variables which may enter into the answers to the above questions. The sum total of the answers to these questions determines the gross investment in inventories, number of stockouts, amount of storage space required, etc. Thus, while the decisions made for any one stock-keeping unit may not be of crucial importance to the conduct and profitability of a business, in sum total these decisions are of great importance.

In view of the importance of these decisions it is understandable that top executives frequently assume direct responsibility for item-by-item inventory decisions. In this manner the top executive can maintain great flexibility, drawing upon his own experience in terms of knowledge of the market, availability of capital, lead-time variables, and the like. Of course, as metals service centers increase in size it is no longer possible for the top executive to *directly* take care of these ordering decisions, and it is necessary to think in terms of the establishment of policies to cover inventory management decisions. It is here that inventory theory provides a means of attaining a balance among conflicting inventory management objectives. In themselves, for example, the objectives of attaining the minimum direct material cost, minimizing the number of stockouts, and minimizing invested capital, are all worthy goals. Unfortunately, these goals conflict with one another, and it is one of the purposes of inventory theory to point a way out of this dilemma.

current inventory management practices in the industry

A picture of the current inventory management practices in the industry is provided by the inventory management research study conducted during 1963-1964. As part of this study, questionnaires were sent to members of the Steel Service Center Institute to gather data concerning inventory record-keeping methods, the manner in which ordering decisions were reached, and types of inventory management problems. The following overall description of inventory practices is provided from the summary of these questionnaire responses.

1. *Nearly ninety percent are using one or another of the manual inventory record-keeping systems (such as Kardex, Acme-Visible, Post Index, or loose-leaf books).*
2. *Fifty-four percent of the respondents are using a reorder point. In most instances this is based upon "a given number of days of normal demand for all items."*
3. *Eight percent of the respondents, or a total of 18 companies, reported that they calculated a "standard cost of possession figure."*
4. *Thirty-nine percent of the companies replied that they used either EOQ formulae or "cost of possession balanced against quantity extras costs," in determining order quantities. These figures indicate that many of the companies which did NOT indicate the calculation of a "cost of possession" figure were nevertheless using an inventory holding cost figure for purposes of order-quantity calculations.*
5. *Sixty-one percent of the respondents determine order quantities only on the basis of "historical records and averages," and/or "turnover goals."*
6. *Forecasting is largely by estimates from salesmen and sales executives and/or other executives, adjusted for current demand or latest sales information.*
7. *Thirty-four percent of the respondents indicated that their present or forward planning included the purchase or lease of a computer or other data-processing equipment. Seventy-one percent of the companies with gross annual sales of over ten million dollars were represented among those planning changes.*

The overall summary of the current inventory management questionnaires indicates a wide diversity of practices. The study also revealed a growing concern for attaining better management of inventories. This was evidenced by the number of companies whose present or forward plans included the purchase or lease of a computer, and is further emphasized by the number of companies whose questionnaire replies indicated that they were seeking better means of decision-making in terms of order quantities and establishment of reorder points.

historical background of inventory theory development

The first known published lot-size formula is credited to a man by the name of Harris, of the Westinghouse Electric and Manufacturing Company. While the determination of the economic *production* lot size was the purpose for his formula, it contained essentially the same variables as are found in many of today's economic order quantity (EOQ) formulae. From this early beginning there was continued interest in lot-size formulae up through the 1920's. One of the stimulants for this interest was the inventory depression of the early 1920's. During 1919-1920 there had been a speculative boom in inventories, and in 1921 the inevitable inventory adjustment took place. One author wrote: "Inventories which had made men rich in the preceding period bankrupted them now. Forced sales, cut prices, liquidations, were rife."[1]

Much of the inventory theory development during this period was pointed toward the development of various formulae as an attempted means of balancing the advantages and disadvantages of holding large and small inventories. In 1928, R. C. Davis presented his paper, "Economic Purchase Quantities," to the Management Section of ASME,[2] suggesting a lot-size formula for use in determining economic *purchase* quantities. In 1931, Fairfield E. Raymond published his full-length book dealing with economic production and purchase quantities. This scholarly book is of interest because of the insights it gives into the conceptual problems which accompanied the development and use of the early lot-size models. Raymond discussed at some length what he believed to be unjustifiable resistance to the use of lot-size formulas. Much of the resistance centered around the difficulties in determining the appropriate interest rate, problems of overhead accounting, and the requirement to use mathematical calculations. He pointed out that:

> During this period of development in scientific methods of management, however, it is quite evident that the tendency has been to attack each phase of manufacture as an individual problem in accordance with the exigencies of the situation, without any particular regard to the manner in which the fundamentals underlying each phase may be re-

---

[1]Thomson M. Whiten, *The Theory of Inventory Management* (Princeton, New Jersey: Princeton University Press, 1953)

[2]R. C. Davis, "Determination of Minimum-Cost Purchase Quantities," *Transactions of the American Society of Mechanical Engineers*, Vol. 49-50, Part II, Management Section, pp. 41-44.

lated in a comprehensive and properly integrated scheme for the conduct of all manufacturing activities.[3]

While Raymond presented some compelling arguments for the use of lot-size formulae, there is little evidence that his or other formulae were widely used in industry. It was not until the early 1950's that there developed a renewed interest in lot-size formulae and other applications of inventory theory.

recent theory development and the role of the computer

There are a number of reasons to account for the renewed interest in the application of inventory theory. One author, after commenting that EOQ formulae had gone into eclipse in the 1930's and 1940's, suggested that the computer was the primary reason for the renewed interest in such formulae in the 1950's. Others have suggested that the increased use of "return on invested capital" as a criterion of business performance helped focus attention on the inventory problem. In addition, inventory theory proved of interest to those in the fields of operations research and management science. In 1957 one author stated that: "More operations research has been directed toward inventory control than toward any other problem area in business and industry. Applications to military inventory problems are becoming increasingly numerous as well. For this reason there are more models available for this class of problems than for any other."[4]

Kenneth Arrow, a highly respected economic theorist, commented on the nature of the inventory models which were being developed in the 1950's. It was his opinion that what distinguished "modern inventory theory" was not the addition of new elements into the theory so much as the manner in which the cost and supply and demand factors were interrelated. He stated:

It is the integration of those elements into consistent wholes, and the determination of optimal policies for models encompassing numerous features, that have been the focus of current research in inventory theory.[5]

---

[3]Fairfield E. Raymond, *Quantity and Economy in Manufacture* (New York: McGraw-Hill Book Co., Inc., 1931), p. 4.

[4]C. West Churchman, Russell L. Ackoff, and E. Leonard Arnoff, *Introduction to Operations Research* (New York: John Wiley and Sons, Inc., 1957) p. 426.

[5]Kenneth Arrow, Samuel Karlen, and Herbert Scarf, *Studies in the Mathematical Theory of Inventory and Production* (Stanford, California: Stanford University Press, 1958), p. 14.

This same author further pointed out the stimulus of the computer when he stated:

> The acceptability of a solution is thus relative to computing technology. With modern developments, straightforward simulation of intricate situations with little or no loss in essential features is sometimes possible so that descriptive solutions are possible with little abstraction or preliminary mathematical analysis.[6]

reduction in the cost of calculations

In general, the more refined the decision-making process, the greater is the expense in its use. The sought-after goal is what one economist has referred to as an "optimally imperfect decision,"—which: "requires that the marginal cost of additional information gathering or more refined calculation be equal to its marginal (expected) gross yield."[7] This statement is of interest because it helps explain why the computer is one of the important reasons for the increased use of inventory control techniques. As pointed out by Forrester:

> In the last fifteen years the cost of arithmetic computation has fallen by a factor of 10,000 or more in the areas where the digital computers can be used in their most efficient modes of operation.[8]

With each increase in speed and memory capacity, the cost of calculations has decreased, and hence the "optimally imperfect decisions" are moving continually in the direction of more refined decision-making processes.

computer not a necessity

While a computer greatly facilitates the computational requirements in the application of inventory theory, and while there are a number of inventory control systems specifically built around the use of a computer, it should not be inferred that a computer is a *necessary* requirement for the usefulness or application of inventory theory and control. In fact, there are a number of good reasons for seeking the

---

[6]*Ibid.*, p. 17.

[7]William J. Baumol and Richard E. Quandt, "Rules of Thumb and Optimally Imperfect Decisions," *The American Economic Review*, Vol. LIV, No. 2, Part I. March, 1964, p. 23.

[8]Jay W. Forrester, *Industrial Dynamics* (New York: John Wiley and Sons, Inc. 1961), p. 18.

application of inventory theory *in advance* of the installation of a computer. One author has stated the case as follows:

> As long as ordering decisions involve judgment they cannot be made mechanically; but when mathematical decision rules are used, mechanization becomes possible. Thus, the optimal ordering rules provided by operations research may lead to a double payoff through better inventory decisions and higher potential for mechanization, provided that mechanization can be done economically.[9]

The development of appropriate decision-making cost information is another benefit which will be of great use for a potential computer application. One may find a number of testimonials similar to the following:

> Despite the difficulty in measuring cost—and indeed because of such difficulty—it is eminently worthwhile to look at the lot-size problem explicitly formulated. The value of an analytic solution does not rest solely on one's ability to plug in precise cost data to get an answer. An analytic solution often helps clarify questions of principle, even with only crude data available for use.[10]

Companies which today cannot justify the purchase or lease of a computer, even if used in a coordinated system including inventory control, order processing, payroll, sales analysis, cost analysis, etc., may find economic justification for a computer within a relatively few years.

In summary, then, irrespective of the present or future feasibility of a computer installation in any given company, there are a number of good reasons for acquiring an understanding of inventory theory. Such an understanding provides an opportunity for an analytical evaluation of inventory management variables. Through this evaluation it is possible to analyze present inventory management practices and to obtain valuable guidance for purposes of establishing inventory policy to guide the determination of order quantities, reorder points, gross inventory investment, etc.

organization of the text

We begin in Chapter 2 by addressing ourselves to an inventory problem which is extremely simple and correspondingly unrealistic.

---

[9]Fred Hannsmann, *Operations Research in Production and Inventory Control* (New York: John Wiley & Sons, Inc., 1962), p. 97.

[10]John F. Magee, *Production Planning and Inventory Control* (New York: McGraw-Hill Book Company, Inc., 1958), p. 45.

In Chapter 3 we introduce an added complexity, increasing the realism of the problem somewhat. In Chapter 4 we introduce further complexities and make the problem still more realistic. Through Chapter 4, however, we have avoided dealing with the inventory problem familiar to metals service center managers. Our purpose in this deliberate shying away from the familiar problem is two-fold: 1) by dealing with a hypothetical rather than a concrete case we can portray more effectively the *general* inventory problem and thus make more fully apparent, in later chapters, the ways in which the metals inventory problem is unique; and 2) by avoiding the metal inventory problem at the outset we can force ourselves to take a fresh look at the inventory problem, and to set aside, for the moment, preconceived notions about that problem, based on our own experience.

In Chapters 2, 3 and 4 we assume that the demand for the product whose inventory we want to manage is given, just as we assume that its delivered cost is given. In real metals inventory systems this datum —the demand—is never given, and the success with which the inventory system is managed is heavily dependent upon the quality of the demand forecast. In chapter 5, therefore, the subject of forecasting is examined.

In Chapter 6 we finally address ourselves to the metals inventory problem. We explore the metals inventory system and identify those features of that system which will enable us to develop a relatively simple procedure for determining optimum inventory policy either by hand or by means of an automatic data processing system.

In Chapters 7 and 8 we examine costs and their relationships to optimum policy, and we pursue further a practicable procedure for determining optium policy.

In Chapter 9 we summarize the complete *algorithm* or *procedure* for determining optimum policy in the management of metals inventories, and we explore some aspects of computerized systems.

It is the expectation of the authors that a reader who is famliiar with inventory management, who is reasonably well grounded in mathematics, and who has some knowledge of statistics can employ this text as a self-instructional affair with relative ease. Those not so equipped should expect that this text, like most texts, is best employed in conjunction with some formal classroom study of the subject. It is our hope that while this text may only serve to give the top executive some familiarity with the theory underlying a sophisticated inventory management strategy, it will help provide the operating manager with an intimate, working knowledge of the subject. In an economy grown increasingly complex and dynamic, judgment needs to be buttressed with knowledge based on rigorous analysis. The purpose of this text is to facilitate the acquisition of that knowledge in the important field of metals inventory management.

2 a simple inventory problem with no uncertainties and without quantity extras

demand for item A

A RETAILER STOCKS UNITS of Item A for resale to his customers. The demand for units of Item A has been constant at 1 unit per day during the recent past and the retailer is confident that this demand rate will not change. Thus, there are no uncertainties with respect to demand, and demand per year is for 365 units of Item A (DPY = 365).*

lead time for replenishment of item A

Lead time—the time which elapses between the placement of an order for replenishing his stock of Item A and the receipt of the new shipment—has been constant at 2 days per lead time period and the retailer is confident that the lead time will not change. Thus there are no uncertainties with respect to lead time, and lead time is 2 days (LT = 2).

delivered cost of item A

The retailer pays $500 per unit of Item A received from his suppliers, regardless of the number of units he orders at one time. Thus, there are no quantity extras and the cost per unit is $500 (CPU = $500).

cost of possession

Holding an inventory of units of Item A costs money. The factors that influence the cost of possession will demand attention later.

---

*For added convenience in reading this text, a symbol glossary is provided following the Table of Contents.

For the moment let us assume that the retailer charges himself each year, for cost accounting purposes, 20% of his average investment in inventory during the year. For example, with an average inventory level of 20 units of Item A, our retailer would have invested in inventory, on the average, $500 x 20 = $10,000. His annual holding cost would be: $10,000 x .20 = $2,000.

The retailer figures his cost of possession, therefore, at 20% per year (COP = .20).

ordering cost for item A

The retailer estimates that it costs him $20 to process a purchase order (CPO = $20).

—THE NATURE OF THE INVENTORY PROBLEM UNDER CERTAINTY, WITHOUT QUANTITY EXTRAS—

The optimum inventory management policy can, in general, be expressed in terms of 3 *specifications:*

1. *The optimum reorder point, R*
2. *The optimum order quantity, Q*
3. *The optimum frequency of policy review*

As we will see in the next two chapters, selecting these 3 specification for a particular product results from an analysis of the following factors:

1. *Annual holding cost, AHC*
2. *Annual ordering cost, AOC*
3. *Annual stockout cost, ASC*
4. *Annual materials cost, AMC*
5. *The rate of change of the preceding 4 factors, and the rate of change of demand and lead time*

We will see further, in the next two chapters, that selecting the optimum reorder point, R, and the optimum order quantity, Q, may involve a search for the best combination of R and Q. That is, it may not be possible to determine the optimum R independently of the optimum Q, and then knowing the optimum R to select the optimum Q. Instead it may be necessary to search for the optimum reorder point and the optimum order quantity simultaneously.

In the inventory problem under certainty, however, no changes are expected. Therefore the last of the five factors above does not enter into our analysis. Furthermore, where there are no uncertainties stockouts can be easily and economically avoided, so factor 3 above does not enter into the analysis.

In our retailer's inventory problem there are no quantity extras, so factor 4 drops out.

Our problem under certainty, and without quantity extras, is now quite simple. We have only to find the optimum R and the optimum Q by "balancing" annual holding cost and annual ordering cost.

the optimum order point for item A

In the inventory problem under certainty, and without quantity extras, we can always determine the optimum reorder point independently of the optimum order quantity and vice versa. Our retailer's system will demonstrate this.

demand during lead time. The number of units our retailer expects to sell during the lead time period is 2 units; lead time is certain to be 2 days, and the demand is for 1 unit per day, so demand during lead time is 2 units (DDLT = 2).

If the retailer reorders when his stock level drops to 2 units (i.e., R = 2) he can achieve two desired objectives: 1) he can contribute toward minimizing his holding costs by causing his stock level in Item A to drop to zero, and 2) he can still be certain he will not get caught short.

By reordering at R = 2 the retailer begins his lead time period with an inventory of 2 units. Two days will elapse before his replenishment supply arrives. During those 2 days 2 units will be sold and his supply will be exhausted. Just as he runs out, however, a new supply arrives and a stockout is avoided. Clearly, regardless of the order quantity he selects, a reorder point of 2 is optimal. In this sense the optimum reorder point and the optimum order quantity are independent of each other, in this simple inventory system.

the optimum order quantity for item A

Our problem now is to select the order quantity, Q, which minimizes the sum of: 1) the annual holding cost, AHC, and 2) the annual ordering cost, AOC.

We have selected a reorder point which causes the inventory level to drop to zero just as a replenishment supply arrives. When the re-

plenishment supply arrives the inventory level will rise to the amount
of the order quantity. Therefore our inventory curve, as time passes,
could have the shape shown in Fig. 2-1.

Figure 2-1

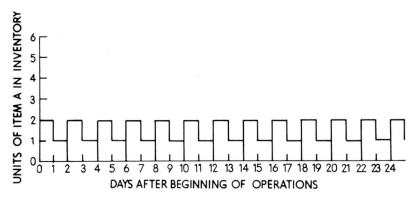

Since withdrawals from inventory are in discrete units our inventory curve is a stair-step affair like that shown in Figure 2-1—a step
resulting from the withdrawal of one unit.

Let us "idealize" our inventory curve, smoothing out the steps
for convenience, as shown in Fig 2-2.

Figure 2-2

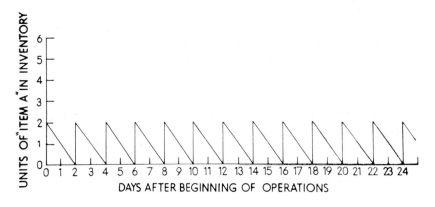

Our idealized inventory curve is a saw-tooth affair rising from a minimum of 0 to a maximum of Q, the order quantity. Our average inventory level, therefore, is ½ the order quantity, or Q/2.

Annual holding cost, AHC, is simply:

$$AHC = Q/2 \text{ x } \$500 \text{ x } 0.20 = \$50Q$$

Our annual ordering cost would be the cost per order (CPO) times the number of orders we will place in a year. The number of orders is simply the demand per year divided by the order quantity (DPY/Q). Thus if we should elect to order 1 unit each time we reorder we will be obliged to place, in the course of 1 year, 365 orders. If we order 10 units each time we reorder we will be obliged to place 36.5 orders per year, etc.

Our annual ordering cost, AOC, then, is:

$$AOC = 365/Q \text{ x } \$20 = \$7300/Q$$

. . . and total annual inventory cost, TAC—ignoring the annual cost of materials—would be the sum of annual holding cost and annual ordering cost, or:

$$TAC = AHC + AOC = \$50Q + \$7300/Q$$

To see how our costs behave as the order quantity is varied let us determine the three costs AHC, AOC and TAC corresponding to order quantities of 4, 6, 18 and 20 (see Table 2-1).

Table 2-1

Order quantity (Q)	4	6	18	20
AHC ($50Q)	$200	$300	$900	$1000
AOC ($7300/Q)	1825	1217	406	365
TAC (AHC + AOC)	$2025	$1517	$1306	$1365

It is apparent from Table 2-1 that the optimum order quantity, that associated with the minimum TAC, is greater than Q = 4 and less than Q = 20 units. Our TAC curve is, in fact, somewhat U-shaped, as shown in Figure 2-3.

Figure 2-3 shows graphically what we know intuitively: that as we order in large order quantities our annual holding cost increases and our annual ordering cost decreases.

Figure 2-3

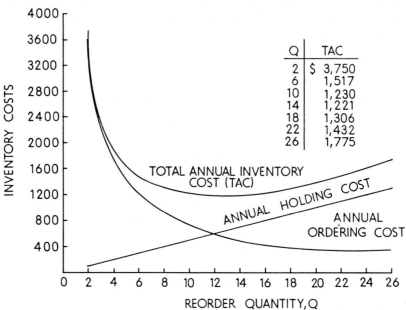

Q	TAC
2	$ 3,750
6	1,517
10	1,230
14	1,221
18	1,306
22	1,432
26	1,775

A most important point to observe here is that as we increase our order quantity, a unit at a time, the annual holding cost rises uniformly. Thus, if we increase Q from 2 to 3—a unit of increase—AHC rises $50; and similarly if we increase Q from 19 to 20—also a unit increase —our AHC rises $50. However, increasing Q from 19 to 20 yields only a $19 reduction in annual ordering cost whereas increasing Q from 2 to 3 yields a $1217 reduction in annual ordering cost.

As a result, unit increases in Q yield substantial reductions in total annual cost *initially*, but as we continue increasing Q each successive unit increase yields less reduction in total annual cost. We soon reach the point where further increases in Q do not yield enough annual ordering cost saving to compensate for the added annual holding cost.

The order quantity corresponding to this point is the Q which minimizes TAC, and hence is the optimum order quantity.

a general EOQ model

To find this optimum Q we could, referring to Figure 2-3, calculate values for TAC associated with all other values of Q between 6 and 18 and simply select the Q which yields a minimum TAC.

A better strategy, however, would be to develop a "general model" for the optimum order quantity. To do this we need to develop the general model for TAC. For the general model, annual holding cost is:

$$AHC = Q/2 \times CPU \times COP$$

Note: For our retailer's system this was: $Q/2 \times \$500 \times 0.2 = \$50Q$.

And for the general model, annual ordering cost is:

$$AOC = DPY/Q \times CPO$$

Note: For our retailer's system this was: $365/Q \times \$20 = \$7300/Q$.

Therefore, our general total annual cost model is:

$$TAC = AHC + AOC = (Q/2 \times CPU \times COP) + (DPY/Q \times CPO)$$

To derive a model or formula for the economic order quantity from the expression above we need to resort to calculus. How we employ calculus to develop the model is not crucial; those unfamiliar with calculus should feel free to ignore the development, skip ahead and refer only to the *solution* which calculus yields.

If we differentiate TAC in the model above with respect to Q, we get:

$$\frac{dTAC}{dQ} = \frac{CPU \times COP}{2} - \frac{DPY \times CPO}{Q^2}$$

And now if we equate the expression on the right side of the equal sign to zero, and solve it for Q we get:

$$Q = \sqrt{\frac{2 \times CPO \times DPY}{COP \times CPU}} \qquad (2\text{-}1)$$

The model above is generally referred to as the economic order quantity model (EOQ model). Given the cost of ordering, CPO, the annual demand, DPY, the cost of possession, COP, and the delivered cost of the product, CPU, using model (2-1) we can calculate the order quantity, Q, which will minimize the sum of annual ordering cost and annual holding cost. For our retailer this quantity proves to be:

$$Q = \sqrt{\frac{2 \times \$20 \times 365}{0.2 \times \$500}} = 12 \text{ units}$$

the decision rule for minimizing inventory cost for item A

Our retailer's decision rule for minimizing annual inventory cost is:

"When the stock level in Item A drops to 2 units order a new supply of 12 units."

With this policy annual holding cost will equal annual ordering cost (at $Q = 12$ our AHC curve crosses our AOC curve in Figure 2-3) and total annual cost will be a minimum at $1208 per year.

3
a simple inventory problem with uncertainties but without quantity extras

TWO ASPECTS OF THE RETAILER'S inventory problem discussed in the preceding chapter made it simple but unrealistic: 1) no uncertainties with regard to daily demand and lead time; and 2) no price breaks associated with order quantities of varying magnitudes.

In this chapter we will add an element of uncertainty to make the model more realistic and therefore more useful. In the next chapter we will introduce quantity extras.

A wholesaler stocks units of Item B for sale to his retail customers.

demand for item B

The demand per day for Item B, during the past 50 days, was as follows:

0	2	0	2	0	1	3	0	2	0
1	0	1	0	2	0	2	1	0	1
0	1	1	1	3	1	0	3	1	2
0	3	0	0	2	0	3	1	0	1
1	0	2	0	0	2	1	2	1	0

The wholesaler feels this "pattern" of daily demand can be expected to continue and is prepared to base his inventory planning on this recent experience. He makes the following important observations about this demand experience:

1. *Demand in one day never exceeds 3 units.*
2. *There seems to be no seasonal factor operative in his demand pattern.*
3. *On 20 of the 50 days for which he has demand data 0 units were demanded. On 15 of the 50 days 1 unit was demanded; on 10 of the 50 days 2 units were demanded; and on 5 of the 50 days 3 units were demanded.*

By setting up a "demand distribution" the wholesaler gains important insights into his demand pattern (see Table 3-1).

Table 3-1

Demand per day (units)	Number of days with demand of this magnitude	Percent of the days demand was of this magnitude
0	20	40%
1	15	30%
2	10	20%
3	5	10%

If our wholesaler has reason to believe his demand pattern in the future will be like that of the recent past, then the demand pattern shown in Table 3-2 represents his forecast of demand for the days ahead.

Table 3-2

Possible demand per day (units)	Relative frequency of this demand
0	40% of the days ahead
1	30% of the days ahead
2	20% of the days ahead
3	10% of the days ahead

We will want to return to a more thorough analysis of the wholesaler's daily demand distribution forecast, but first let us set forth other characteristics of the wholesaler's inventory system.

lead time for replenishment of item B

Over the past 40 reorder cycles the wholesaler has experienced lead times of the following duration:

3	1	2	1	2	3	2	2
2	2	1	2	3	2	1	3
1	2	2	3	2	2	2	3
3	3	1	1	1	1	3	2
2	2	2	2	3	2	2	1

The wholesaler expects this pattern of lead time duration to continue, and makes the following important observations about his lead time experience:

1. *Lead time never exceeds 3 days' duration.*
2. *There seems to be no seasonal factor operative in the lead time pattern.*
3. *In 10 of the 40 reorder cycles lead time was 1 day in duration; in 20 of the 40 it was 2 days in duration; and in 10 of the 40 it was 3 days in duration.*

By setting up a "lead time distribution" the wholesaler gains important insights into his lead time pattern (see Table 3-3).

Table 3-3

Lead time duration (days)	Number of reorder cycles with lead time duration of this magnitude	Percent of the lead time periods with duration of this magnitude
1	10	25%
2	20	50%
3	10	25%

If our wholesaler has reason to believe his future lead time experience will be like that of the recent past, then the lead time pattern shown in Table 3-4 represents his forecast of lead time in the reorder periods ahead.

Table 3-4

Possible lead time duration (days)	Relative frequency of this lead time duration
1	25%
2	50%
3	25%

Delivered Cost of Item B. As with our retailer in Chapter 2, the delivered cost of the item whose inventory our wholesaler wants to manage is $500 per unit.

Cost of possession for Item B. As with our retailer in Chapter 2, the holding cost which the wholesaler associates with stocking units of Item B is 20% of the average inventory in Item B, per year (COP = .20).

Ordering cost for Item B. As before, the cost of processing one purchase order is $20 (CPO = $20).

—THE NATURE OF THE INVENTORY PROBLEM UNDER UNCERTAINTY WITHOUT QUANTITY EXTRAS—

As was stated in Chapter 2, the optimum inventory policy can, in general, be expressed in terms of 3 specifications:

1. *The optimum reorder point, R*
2. *The optimum order quantity, Q*
3. *The optimum frequency of policy review*

We also observed in the previous chapter that the above 3 specifications for a particular product result from an analysis of:

1. *Annual holding cost, AHC*
2. *Annual ordering cost, AOC*
3. *Annual stockout cost, ASC*
4. *Annual materials cost, AMC*
5. *The rate of change of the preceding 4, and the rate of change of demand and lead time*

If we eliminate quantity extras, then factor 4 does not enter the analysis. Similarly if we assume, as our wholesaler does, that the demand "level" is not changing over time and that the "level" of the lead time duration does not change, then factor 5 does not enter into the analysis.[1].

average daily demand and average lead time for item B

The similarity between the retailer model of Chapter 2 and the wholesaler model goes further. The retailer's daily demand was 1 unit of Item A. If we average the 50 individual daily demands which our wholesaler experienced during the past 50 days we find that the mean or average demand was 1 unit per day, and thus that his demand-per-year forecast would be 365 units (DPY = 365).

Similarly, if we average the 40 lead time data we find that the average lead time duration was 2 days, and thus that the lead time forecast is 2 days (LT = 2).

However, the dissimilarity between the retailer and wholesaler models is of great significance. Our retailer knew with certainty the

---

[1]By a constant demand and a constant lead time "level" we mean that while daily demand is expected to fluctuate between 0 and 3 units, and while lead time duration is expected to fluctuate between 1 and 3 days, the demand and lead time distributions, shown in Table 3-2 and Table 3-4 respectively, are *not* expected to change.

number of units of Item A he would sell tomorrow, and was certain about the duration of lead time. Our wholesaler is *not* certain. While he knows something about the relative likelihood of demands of varying magnitudes and something about the relative likelihood of lead times of varying duration, he cannot be certain about the magnitude of sales tomorrow or any other day, nor about the duration of lead time when he next reorders.

For our wholesaler, avoiding a stockout is easy but it may not be economically wise. In this respect our wholesaler's model differs radically from the retailer model of Chapter 2. Annual stockout cost *does* enter into our determination of the optimum reorder point and the optimum order quantity.

Specifying the optimum inventory policy for Item B, therefore, requires an analysis of:

1. *Annual holding cost, AHC*
2. *Annual ordering cost, AOC*
3. *Annual stockout cost, ASC*

To develop a model for specifying the optimum reorder point and the optimum order quantity for our wholesaler we need some scheme for assessing the probabilities of stockouts of varying magnitudes associated with various possible reorder policies. This requires that we manipulate the data in Tables 3-2 and 3-4. Prior to this however, we would do well to digress for a moment to acquaint ourselves with some rather powerful concepts concerning probability. Specifically we need to acquaint ourselves with:

1. *Probability as relative frequency*
2. *Joint probability*
3. *Expected values*
   Expected demand during lead time
   Expected stockout during lead time
   Expected annual stockout
4. *Cumulative probability*

—SOME FUNDAMENTAL PROBABILITY CONCEPTS—

probability as relative frequency

If we asked someone what the probability of our tossing a tail on one toss of a good coin is, he would probably answer "½." By his answer he would demonstrate that to him "probability" and "rela-

judgment versus rigorous analysis

We could form some judgment about the likelihood of a stock-out during lead time simply by looking at these distributions—that is, without analyzing them carefully.

For example, we observe that with a reorder point of 9 units our wholesaler will never get caught short. This follows from the fact that the maximum lead time he can expect is 3 days, and the maximum demand per day is 3 units. If he reorders when his stock level drops to 9 he will not get caught short.

On the other hand if he lets his stock level in Item B drop to 0 before reordering he can expect to get caught short, *on the average,* 2 units per lead time period. This follows from the fact that the *average* demand is 1 unit per day; the average demand during lead time, therefore, would be 2 units. If, on the average, 2 units are demanded during lead time and we start each lead time period with 0 units on hand (that is, with R = 0) then we can expect to experience, on the average, 2 units' stockout during lead time.

If stocking units of Item B for resale is profitable, then almost certainly a reorder policy which yields an average stockout of 2 units per lead time period is not wise. Using "judgment," then, we might select some reorder point higher than 0 and less than or equal to 9.

But 'higher than 0 and equal to or less than 9' is not very specific. We are not content with a reorder policy based on such superficial observation. We want to select the *optimum* policy, and this requires rather exhaustive analysis of the information at our disposal.

To do this we need to know the probability of a *demand during lead time* of 9 units, the probability of 8 units, the probability of 7 units etc. That is, we need a *demand during lead time distribution*—a probability distribution similar to those of Tables 3-5 and 3-6 but one telling us the probabilities associated with various possible demands during lead time.

probability distribution for demand
during lead time for item B

Now that we are equipped with a knowledge of joint probabilities, we can develop such a probability distribution. Let us begin by determining the probability of a demand during lead time for 9 units —the maximum possible demand during lead time.

We need to know the joint probability of the combination of events:

a. A lead time of 3 days' duration (probability of 3 = .25), *combined with*

b. A demand for 3 units on the first day (probability of 3 = .10), *combined with*

c. A demand for 3 units on the second day (probability of 3 = .10) *combined with*

d. A demand for 3 units on the third day (probability of 3 = .10)

This would be simply the product of the probabilities of the 4 individual events set forth above; that is:

$$\text{(Probability of a)} \quad \text{x} \quad \text{(Probability of b)} \quad \text{x} \quad \text{(Probability of c)} \quad \text{x} \quad \text{(Probability of d)}$$

... or:

$$0.25 \text{ x } 0.10 \text{ x } 0.10 \text{ x } 0.10 = 0.00025$$

Let us round this answer to 0.0003. The first datum for our probability distribution for demand during lead time, therefore, is 0.0003: the probability of a demand during lead time of 9 units.

It must occur to us that a demand during lead time of 8 units is also possible. We could have a demand during lead time of 8 units in the following way:

Lead time = 3 days
Demand on the first day: 3 units
Demand on the second day: 3 units
Demand on the third day: 2 units
Total demand = 8 units

What is the probability of this combination of events? As before, this would be the product of the probabilities of the individual events:

$$0.25 \text{ x } 0.10 \text{ x } 0.10 \text{ x } 0.20 = .0005$$

But notice that this is not the probability of a demand during lead time of 8 units. This is the probability of a demand during lead time of 8 units *given that those 8 units are demanded in the following sequence:* first day—3 units; second day—3 units; third day —2 units.

A demand during lead time of 8 could also occur in the following sequence:

> Lead time = 3 days
> Demand on the first day: 3 units
> Demand on the second day: 2 units
> Demand on the third day: 3 units
>   Total demand = 8 units

And obviously there is a third sequence which could yield a demand during lead time of 8 units:

> Lead time = 3 days
> Demand on the first day: 2 units
> Demand on the second day: 3 units
> Demand on the third day: 3 units
>   Total demand = 8 units

The probability of the second sequence above is:

$$0.25 \times 0.10 \times 0.20 \times 0.10 = 0.0005$$

And the probability of the third sequence above is:

$$0.25 \times 0.20 \times 0.10 \times 0.10 = 0.0005$$

The "total probability" of a demand during lead time of 8 units would be the sum of the 3 individual probabilities, or:[2]

$$.0005 + .0005 + .0005 = .0015$$

We now have a second datum for our demand during lead time probability distribution. We could go on using this same method to determine the probabilities of 7 units, 6 units, etc., thru 0 units, and thus complete our demand during lead time distribution.[3]

The resulting probability distribution would be as shown in Table 3-7.

---

[2] This is apparent if we think once again of probability as the equivalent of relative frequency. The relative frequency of the first sequence above which yields a demand during lead time of 8 units is 5 out of every 10,000 times. But five out of every 10,000 lead time periods we expect one or the other of various combinations of events which yield a demand during lead time of 8 units. The probability of a demand during lead time of 8, then, is .0015.

[3] For a more practicable way to do this when the distributions we are working from are more involved, see Appendix A.

Table 3-7

Possible demand during lead time (units)	Probability of this demand
0	.1960
1	.2310
2	.2260
3	.1797
4	.0935
5	.0477
6	.0190
7	.0053
8	.0015
9	.0003

probability of a stockout—cumulative probability

From our demand during lead time distribution in Table 3-7 we can easily determine the probability of a stockout during lead time associated with various possible reorder policies.

A stockout can only occur during lead time. If we begin our lead time period with 9 units on hand, as we observed earlier, we will not get caught short since 9 units is the maximum possible demand during lead time. Therefore, the probability of a stockout during lead time, associated with a policy of reordering when the stock level drops to 9, is zero.

With a reorder point of 8, however, we *can* get caught short. What is the probability of a stockout during lead time associated with a policy of reordering when the stock level drops to 8 units? The event which would cause a stockout, given that R = 8, is: "a demand during lead time for 9 units." The probability of this event is .0003. Therefore the probability of a stockout during lead time associated with a reorder policy of R = 8 is .0003.

What is the probability of a stockout during lead time associated with a reorder point of 7 units? Two events can occur which could cause a stockout with this policy:

1. *A demand during lead time for 9 units, or*
2. *A demand during lead time for 8 units*

The probability of *one or the other* of these two events is:

$$.0003 + .0015 = .0018$$

This becomes apparent as we think once again of probability as relative frequency. Three out of every 10,000 lead time periods we expect a demand during lead time of 9 units. Fifteen out of every 10,000 lead time periods we expect a demand during lead time of 8 units. Therefore 18 out of every 10,000 lead time periods we expect a demand during lead time in excess of 7 units, and hence the probability of a stockout during lead time associated with a reorder point of R = 7 is .0018.

These are called *cumulative probabilities*, and the cumulative probability associated with 6, for example, means: "The probability of a demand during lead time in excess of 6 units."

Table 3-8 is the demand during lead time probability distribution of Table 3-7 with a column added for cumulative probabilities.

Table 3-8

Possible demand during lead time (also reorder point)	Probability of this demand	Cumulative probability (probability that demand during lead time will be greater than this) P(DDLT > R)
0	.1960	.8040
1	.2310	.5730
2	.2260	.3470
3	.1797	.1673
4	.0935	.0738
5	.0477	.0261
6	.0190	.0071
7	.0053	.0018
8	.0015	.0003
9	.0003	.0000

The probabilities in this added column are simply the sums of those probabilities listed in the middle column—those pertaining to demands during lead time greater than the reorder point under consideration.

Observe that we have begun to view the numbers in the first column of our demand during lead time distribution as "possible reorder points" as well as "possible demands during lead time." The expression "P(DDLT > R)" in the last column of Table 3-8 should be interpreted to mean "the probability that demand during lead time will be greater than the reorder point, R."

We observed earlier that for a rigorous analysis we are obliged to know not only *the probabilities of stockouts*, given a variety of possible reorder points, but also the *probable magnitudes of stockouts during lead time associated with a variety of possible reorder points*.

We can get at this additional element from the distribution of Table 3-8, but first we need to acquaint ourselves with a concept of major importance in management decision making: the concept of *expected value. Expected value: Expected Payoff; Expected Demand; Expected Lead Time; Expected Demand During Lead Time; and Expected Stockout.*

The "expected value" of a decision under uncertainty is the sum of the consequences of that decision discounted by the probabilities that those consequences will occur. For example, suppose Pete was given the opportunity to play the following game:

A coin will be tossed. If it turns up tails Pete wins $10. If it turns up heads Pete wins nothing.

Associated with Pete's *decision to play* is the *expected payoff:*

$$.5 \times \$10 = \$5$$

Expected payoff, then, is the *average* payoff to Pete per game, assuming Pete plays the game a large number of times.

Let's make the game a bit more realistic:

A coin will be tossed. If it turns up tails Pete wins $10. If it turns up heads Pete loses $7. For the privilege of playing the game, however, Pete must pay $1.

If Pete decides to play and a tail is tossed he is $9 ahead. If a head is tossed he loses $8. Proceeding as before, associated with Pete's *decision to play* is the *expected payoff:*

Outcome	Probability		Consequence	
Tail	.5	×	$9	= $4.50
Head	.5	×	$-8	= -4.00
			Sum	= $ .50

The expected payoff to Pete is $.50.

Thinking again in terms of relative frequency, if Pete plays the game 100 times we would *expect* the following experience (but not, of course, in this order):

Outcome	Number of Times		Consequence	
Tail	50	×	$9	= $450
Head	50	×	-8	= -400
				$ 50

We would expect Pete to be $50 ahead in 100 games and his average or expected payoff per game is therefore $50/100 = $.50.

Notice that in one game (in one toss) Pete has an expected payoff of $.50, and yet he will never win $.50 in one game. In any one game Pete will either win $9 or he will lose $8. However, this fact does not detract from the importance of the concept of expected payoff.

Expected value involves "discounting"—discounting a consequence by the probability of the event which yields that consequence. It is somewhat analogous to discounting to get *present value*.

If I invest $5580 at 6% compounded annually it will grow to $10,000 in 10 years. If I "give up" my $5580 today with the expectation of receiving $10,000 10 years from now I am paying $5580 for the right to receive $10,000 in 10 years. Thus if I make the investment, then apparently I assess the value of the right to receive $10,000 in 10 years at $5580 or higher.

If this is my state of mind, one might say that to determine the present value of the right to receive $10,000 in 10 years I am "discounting" the $10,000 by a factor of 0.558:

$$\$10,000 \text{ x } 0.558 = \$5580$$

Thus I am discounting the *consequence* of the *decision to invest* to get its present value. Present-value tables—standard equipment among financial analysts—are simply tables of discount factors.

In a similar way, in decision problems under uncertainty, we discount the consequences of events (outcomes) by the probabilities that they will occur.

For example, the daily demand distribution for Item B was as follows:

Possible demand in a day (units)	Probability
0	.4
1	.3
2	.2
3	.1

Four events (demands) are possible in this demand distribution. If we multiply the consequences of these events by the possibilities of their occurrence and sum the products we can get the *expected daily demand*, much as we got Pete's expected payoff:

Event		Probability		
0	×	.4	=	0.0
1	×	.3	=	0.3
2	×	.2	=	0.4
3	×	.1	=	0.3
		Sum		1.0

By this procedure we are really getting a *weighted average* and the result is the same, of course, as it would be if we simply added up the individual days' demands in the sample of 50 days of demand experience from which our daily demand distribution was developed and divided by 50. Average or expected demand per day is 1 unit.

From our lead time distribution we can get the *expected duration of lead time* for Item B:

Event		Probability		
1	×	.25	=	0.25
2	×	.50	=	1.00
3	×	.20	=	0.75
			Sum	2.00

And the average or expected lead time is 2 days' duration.

Since the expected lead time is 2 days and the expected demand per day is 1 unit, the expected demand during lead time is 2 units (DDLT = 2).

Proceeding in this same fashion we can determine *expected stockout during lead time* associated with a variety of reorder policies. *Expected stockout with reorder point R = 8.* If we reorder at R = 8, *one* event can occur which would yield a stockout: a demand for 9 units during lead time. If 9 units are demanded we will get caught short 1 unit during lead time. The *complete* set of events associated with a reorder point of 8, their probabilities, (obtained from Table 3-8) and the sum of the products of their consequences and their probabilities give us the expected units short or the *expected stockout* associated with this reorder policy:

Event (units demanded during lead time)	Probability		Consequence		
0 1 2 3 4 5 6 7 8	9997	×	0	=	0
9...0003		×	1	=	.0003
			Sum	=	.0003

The expected stockout during lead time associated with a reorder policy of R = 8, therefore, is .0003 units.

Expected stockout with reorder point R = 7. If we reorder at R = 7 *two* events can occur which would yield a stockout. The complete set of events associated with a reorder of 7, their probabilities and the product of their consequences and their probabilities are:

Event (units demanded during lead time)	Probability	Consequence			
0 1 2 3 4 5 6 7	.9982	×	0	=	.0000
8	.0015	×	1	=	.0015
9	.0003	×	2	=	.0006
			Sum	=	.0021

The expected stockout during lead time associated with a reorder policy of R = 7, therefore, is .0021 units.

Continuing in this way we could determine the expected stockouts associated with all 10 reorder policies. These are shown in Table 3-9.

Table 3-9

Possible demand during lead time (also reorder point)	Probability of this demand	Cumulative probability (probability that demand during lead time will be greater) P(DDLT > R)	Expected stockout during lead time E(DDLT > R)
0	.1960	.8040	2.0000
1	.2310	.5730	1.1864
2	.2260	.3470	0.6234
3	.1797	.1673	0.2764
4	.0935	.0738	0.1091
5	.0477	.0261	0.0353
6	.0190	.0071	0.0092
7	.0053	.0018	0.0021
8	.0015	.0003	0.0003
9	.0003	.0000	0.0000

E(DDLT > R), in the final column of Table 3-9, should be interpreted to mean "the expected amount by which the demand during lead time exceeds the reorder point"; that is, the expected stockout *in units short* during lead time, associated with a particular reorder policy.

A practical method for determining expected stockout during lead time. There is a better way of determining E(DDLT > R), one which involves less computation. Observe the following:

Let P(R) represent the probability of a demand for R units during lead time. The second column in Table 3-9 now represents values for P(R). In calculating values for E(DDLT > R) in the procedure above we were doing the following: (See Table 3-10)

Table 3-10

E(DDLT > 9) = 0
E(DDLT > 8) = 1 × P(9) = 1 × (.0003) = .0003
E(DDLT > 7) = 2 × P(9) + 1 × P(8) = 2 × (.0003) + 1 × (.0015) = .0021
E(DDLT > 6) = 3 × P(9) + 2 × P(8) + 1 × P(7) = 3 × (.0003) + 2 × (.0015) + 1 × (.0003) = .0092
etc.

Now, notice that in calculating values for the cumulative probabilities in the third column of Table 3-9, we proceeded as follows: (See Table 3-11)

Table 3-11

P(DDLT > 9) = 0
P(DDLT > 8) = P(9) = .0003
P(DDLT > 7) = P(9) + P(8) = .0003 + .0015 = .0018
P(DDLT > 6) = P(9) + P(8) = .0003 + .0015 + .0053 = .0071
etc.

Notice that the successive values of E(DDLT > R) in Table 3-10 are simply the successive *sums* of the values for P(DDLT > R) in Table 3-11.

We observe, therefore, that we can get the expected stockout during lead time associated with a particular reorder point, R, by simply adding to the cumulative probability associated with R the cumulative probabilities associated with all reorder points greater than R, as shown in Table 3-12.

Table 3-12

E(DDLT > 9) = P(DDLT > 9) = 0
E(DDLT > 8) = P(DDLT > 9) + P(DDLT > 8) = .0003
           P(DDLT > 9) + P(DDLT > 8) + P(DDLT > 7) = .0021
etc.

We now have a simple method for determining E(DDLT > R), given the cumulative probabilities associated with all reorder points of magnitude R and greater.

To make our simpler method more general, however, we must introduce one added element.

In our wholesaler's demand during lead time distribution we are comparing the consequences of policies involving reorder points which differ from each other by 1 unit. In real inventory systems this is a luxury. If "reasonable" reorder points range from 1,200 lbs. to 2,000 lbs. for example, we might prefer to compare the 80 possible reorder points which differ from each other by 10 lbs. rather than the 800 which differ from each other by 1 lb.

To see the implications of this, assume that our wholesaler's demand during lead time distribution was as follows:

Possible demand during lead time (also reorder point)	Probability of this demand	Cumulative probability $P(DDLT > R)$
0	.1960	.8040
5	.2310	.5730
10	.2260	.3470
15	.1797	.1673
20	.0935	.0738
25	.0477	.0261
30	.0190	.0071
35	.0053	.0018
40	.0015	.0003
45	.0003	.0000

Using our *initial* method we would calculate expected stockouts during lead time as follows:

Table 3-13

$E(DDLT > 45) = 0$
$E(DDLT > 40) = 5 \times P(45) = 5(.0003) = .0015$
$E(DDLT > 35) = 10 \times P(45) + 5 \times P(40) = .0105$
$E(DDLT > 30) = 15 \times P(45) + 10 \times P(40) + 5 \times P(35) = .0460$

Notice that the values obtained in Table 3-13 above are, in each case, 5 times the values in Table 3-9.

We have shown that if we are comparing alternative reorder points which differ from each other by X units, we can calculate the expected stockout per lead time period associated with a reorder point, R, by adding to the cumulative probability associated with R the cumulative probabilities associated with all reorder points greater than R and multiplying the sum by X.

In real inventory management systems we find that the demand during lead time data required in determining optimum reorder points consists of three columns of data. Using our wholesaler's inventory system as an example the data required appears in Table 3-14.

Table 3-14

Reorder points to be considered	P(DDLT > R)	E(DDLT > R)
0	.8040	2.0000
1	.5730	1.1864
2	.3470	0.6234
3	.1673	0.2764
4	.0738	0.1091
5	.0261	0.0353
6	.0071	0.0092
7	.0018	0.0021
8	.0003	0.0003
9	.0000	0.0000

annual stockout cost, ASC, for item B

Estimating the cost associated with a stockout is a subject we will want to examine in some detail later. For the moment let us assume that our wholesaler figures the total cost to him (chiefly lost profit) resulting from a stockout is $40 per unit stockout (SC = $40).

Since the expected number of units short during lead time associated with a policy of reordering when the stock level drops to 4 is 0.1091, the expected stockout cost during lead time would be:

$$.1091 \text{ x } \$40 = \$4.36$$

Since the expected demand per year divided by the order quantity gives us the expected number of reorder cycles per year, and hence the number of lead times per year, the expected annual stockout cost associated with a policy of reordering when the stock level drops to 4 units would be:

$$ASC = 365/Q \text{ x } .1091 \text{ x } \$40$$

For the more general annual stockout cost model we can write:

$$ASC = DPY/Q \text{ x } E(DDLT > R) \text{ x } SC \qquad (3\text{-}1)$$

interdependence of the optimum order quantity and the optimum reorder point

We observed in Chapter 2 that in the inventory problem under conditions of uncertainty it may not be possible to determine the

optimum reorder point and the optimum order quantity independently, as we did with our retailer's inventory system, but rather that we
may be obliged to search simultaneously for the optimum combination of these two.

This fact is suggested by expression (3-1) above. Clearly annual
stockout cost depends on both Q and R. We will see in a moment
that annual holding cost also depends on both Q and R.

annual holding cost for item B

As before, our wholesaler's annual holding cost will be the
average number of units of Item B in inventory times the cost per
unit times the cost of possession. But what is the average inventory?
Average inventory is no longer simply ½ the order quantity, Q.
Since a stockout is not so easy to avoid, economically, we are probably going to find that carrying some base stock is desirable.[4] In this
event our inventory level will *not* fluctuate between 0 and Q as it
did in our retailer's inventory system under certainty.

To get at our wholesaler's average inventory level let us examine
an idealized curve of his inventory *assuming no stockouts* occur. (see
Figure 3-1).

We know, of course, that the wholesaler's actual inventory curve
would look more like that shown in Figure 3-2, in which an occasional

Figure 3-1

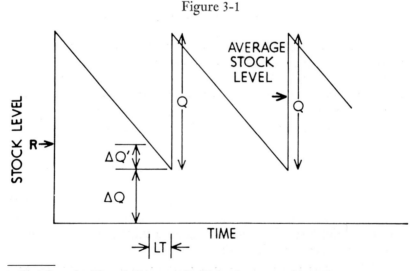

---

[4]Our "base stock" or "safety stock" will be the *excess* of our reorder point over
our *average* demand during lead time.

stockout is expected to occur. If we assume that a stockout will not occur, however, and if we plot our average inventory pattern, with steps smoothed out, it will look much like that of Figure 3-1.

Figure 3-2

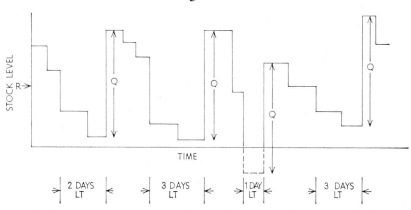

It should be apparent from Figure 3-1 that our average inventory would be:

$$Q/2 + \triangle Q$$

The component of inventory labeled $\triangle Q$ is *always* with us (assuming no stockouts). The *average* of the component which rises above $\triangle Q$ and which fluctuates from $\triangle Q$ to $\triangle Q + Q$ would be simply $Q/2$, so our average inventory would be $Q/2 + \triangle Q$.

Clearly, $\triangle Q$ is $R - \triangle Q'$. But what is $\triangle Q'$? $\triangle Q'$ is the increment of inventory which, on the average, is withdrawn from inventory during lead time, or the expected demand during lead time, DDLT (for Item B DDLT = 2 units). Therefore our average inventory would be:

$$Q/2 + (R - 2) = Q/2 + R - 2$$

To arrive at this expression for average inventory we assumed no stockouts would occur. We know, however, that stockouts probably will occur, and hence our analysis above would seem to be suspect. Observe the following argument, however:

If we assume that a stockout can occur, then during those lead time periods when a stockout does occur the actual withdrawal from inventory, and hence the reduction of the inventory level, will be less than $\triangle Q'$ by an amount equal to the amount demanded but not available. The *average* $\triangle Q$, therefore, would be greater by the stock demanded but not available, and hence our average inventory level throughout the year would seem to be greater than $Q/2 + R - 2$.

But we assume that backordering is permitted in our wholesaler's inventory system—that if a customer's order cannot be filled due to stockout, that customer's order is filled out of the next shipment received. This would mean that following a lead time period when a stockout does occur the inventory level falls short of rising to a level equal to the reorder quantity, Q, by an amount equal to the back-ordered demand.

It develops that the errors in our determination of average inventory level above tend to cancel each other out and the average inventory can be considered to be:

$$Q/2 + R - DDLT$$

Let us continue to develop our wholesaler's model, assuming that backordering is permitted. Later we will discuss the implication of our model when applied to an inventory system in which backordering is not permitted.

If our wholesaler's average inventory is $Q/2 + R - 2$, then his annual holding cost, AHC, would be:

$$AHC = (Q/2 + R - 2) \times \$500 \times .20$$

For the more general model we can write:

$$AHC = (Q/2 + R - DDLT) \times CPU \times COP$$

annual ordering cost for item B

Since we expect our wholesaler to place 365/Q orders per year, his annual ordering cost would be:

$$AOC = 365/Q \times \$20$$

. . . and for the more general model we can write:

$$AOC = DPY/Q \times CPO$$

general model for the inventory system under uncertainty without quantity extras

Total annual cost for Item B, exclusive of materials cost, would be annual stockout cost plus annual holding cost plus annual ordering cost, or: TAC = $[365/Q$ x E(DDLT $>$ R) x \$40] + $[(Q/2 + R - 2)$ x \$500 x .20] + $[365/Q$ x \$20] .... or, for the more general model:

$$TAC = [DPY/Q \text{ x } E(DDLT > R) \text{ x } SC] + [(Q/2 + R - DDLT) \text{ x } CPU \text{ x } COP] + [DPY/Q \text{ x } CPO]$$

Once a reorder point, R, is specified, the quantity E(DDLT $>$ R) is specified by our distribution in Table 3-9. Therefore, for our wholesaler's system there are 2 unknowns on the right side of the equal sign in the model above. Our objective is to find that combination of values for Q and R which causes TAC to be a minimum.

Let us do it first the hard way. Let us simply give R some small value, then calculate TAC from our general TAC model above as Q varies over a wide range of values. Then we can give R a slightly larger value and once again calculate TAC as Q varies over a wide range of values, etc. From our complete system of output data we can select that combination of Q and R which yielded the lowest TAC, and this will be our optimum combination.

In Table 3-17 (at the end of this chapter) are shown values for average inventory, annual shortage, ASC, AHC, AOC, TAC, and TAC Including Annual Materials cost (TACIM) associated with a variety of combinations of Q and R.

the optimum inventory policy for item B

From the TAC column of Table 3-17 it is apparent that total cost is at a minimum of \$1534.07 per year when Q = 13 units and R = 4 units. The wholesaler's decision rule, therefore, for minimizing his total annual inventory cost is:

"When the stock level in Item B drops to 4 units, reorder 13 units."

—SOME FURTHER CHARACTERISTICS OF THE WHOLESALER'S INVENTORY SYSTEM—

We can learn a number of things about inventory systems in general and about our wholesaler's system in particular if we pose a

number of questions, answers to which can be found by working
with the data in table 3-17.

*Optimum policy when the supplier specifies a minimum order
quantity.* Suppose the wholesaler's suppliers refuse to ship fewer than
25 units per order. It is evident from the TAC column of Table 3-17
that total annual costs will now be at a minimum if the wholesaler
moves to a reorder point of 3 rather than 4 units.

Q	R	TAC
25	4	$1805.71
25	3	1803.42

*Optimum order quantity when ordering at less than the optimum
reorder point.* Suppose the last sale—that which immediately precedes
the beginning of our wholesaler's lead time period—reduces the stock
level to 2 units. We have now passed through the reorder point and
reordering at the optimum reorder point of 4 is impossible. Under this
circumstance, is 13 units still the optimum quantity to order?
Obviously it is not:

Q	R	TAC
13	2	$1911.66
18	2	1811.20

The best Q, given a reorder point of 2 units, is a Q of 18.

This should not be surprising. Suppose we were always obliged,
for some reason, to reorder at 2 units. Expected stockout during lead
time is high with a reorder point of R = 2 (see Table 3-17). If we
increase the order quantity we reduce the number of lead time
periods in a year and thus the number of stockout opportunities.
When dealing with very low reorder points the reduction in annual
stockout cost associated with increasing the order quantity more than
compensates for the added annual holding cost.

We will return later to this idea of "trading increased inventory
for reduced stockout opportunity."

Optimum policy to achieve a specified service level. Suppose the
wholesaler insists on a service level of at least 99.72%; that is, he
wants to be able to meet 99.72% of his expected demand of 365
units in a year from off his shelf, without backordering. He would be
prepared, therefore, to experience a stockout of .27% of this demand,
or 1 unit per year.

What reorder policy meets this requirement most economically?

Referring to the column labeled Annual Shortage, in Table 3-17, it is apparent that the following policies meet this service level:

Q	R	TAC
38	4	$2334.02
13	5	1551.18

The better of *these* two policies is, of course, Q = 13 and R = 5. Clearly, however, a service level of this magnitude does not pay. It costs $17.11 more than the optimum policy of Q = 13 and R = 4, ($1551.18 — $1534.09) in which service level is 99.1% (365.0 — 3.1 units of expected stockout divided by 365 = 99.1%).

Optimum policy and turnover. Turnover is commonly employed as a criterion in evaluating whether inventories are too high and hence is a sort of inventory management decision rule. As a *gross* measure by means of which the reasonableness of a multi-product inventory level might be evaluated, turnover has some value. Let us test turnover as a criterion for evaluating alternative inventory policies where only one product is concerned. Let us see first what the rate of turnover is for Item B.

Turnover usually means the number of times per year that the inventory is "replaced" or turned over, and is defined as annual sales divided by average inventory.

In our wholesaler's system, annual sales would be annual demand, since backordering is permitted. Turnover, therefore, would be:

$$DPY/(\text{Average Inventory}) = 365/(Q/2 + R - 2)$$

If our wholesaler employes the optimum reorder policy his turnover will be:

$$365/(13/2 + 4 - 2) = 43 \text{ times per year}$$

Is turnover of this magnitude possible via any other policy? That is, are there other combinations of values for Q and R which would yield a turnover of 43 times per year?

$$365/(Q/2 + R - 2) = 43$$
$$Q/2 + R - 2 = 8.5$$
$$Q + 2R = 21$$
$$Q = 21 - 2R$$

To get at the answer let us solve for Q in terms of R using the final expression above.

Below are listed 5 combinations of values for Q and R, each of which satisfies the equation above and, hence, each of which yields a turnover of 43 times per year:

Q	R	TAC
17	2	$1814
15	3	1605
13	4	1534
11	5	1560
9	6	1676

Only one policy gives both a turnover of 43 and the minimum total annual inventory cost. Therefore, we cannot specify the optimum policy in terms of turnover alone, and we cannot evaluate the propriety of a particular policy solely by reference to the turnover it will yield.

Stockout frequency. If our wholesaler employs the least cost inventory policy for Item B (i.e., Q = 13 and R = 4) how frequently should he expect a stockout? To get at this we reason as follows:

Referring to Table 3-9 we see that the probability of a stockout during lead time (the cumulative probability) with a policy of reordering at R = 4 is .0738. This means that our wholesaler can expect a stockout 7.38% of his lead time periods.

Since he expects about 28 lead time periods per year (365/13) he can expect about 2 stockouts per year (7.38% of 28).

This does NOT mean, of course, that our wholesaler *will* experience 2 stockouts each year. It means that the average or expected stockout frequency is twice per year. *Under conditions of uncertainty the best we can do is to estimate probabilities of events, assess the monetary value of their consequences and base our decision on expected values. Whether we apply numerical measures to the probabilities and the consequences of events we do, in fact, employ this practice whenever we make decisions on any basis other than caprice.*

Table 3-15

Q	R	TAC	Percent excess of TAC over TAC with optimum policy
11	3	$1680	9.5%
16	6	1665	8.5%

Sensitivity analysis. In any inventory system we are interested in knowing the sensitivity of the system to changes either in costs or in deviation from the optimum policy.

To assess the sensitivity of our wholesaler's system to deviations from the optimum policy, let us compare the TAC associated with policies ranging from Q = 11, R = 3 to Q = 16, R = 6 (see Table 3-15).

As the final column in Table 3-15 indicates, the excess costs associated with deviations of this magnitude from the optimum reorder policy are significant.

How about a more modest deviation? Why not, for example, adopt the policy: Q = 12, R = 6?

By adopting this policy we reduce expected stockouts from 2 per year to once every 5 years (the probability of a stockout during lead time associated with R = 6 is .0071; .0071 x 365/12 = .2, approximately; thus the number of stockouts per year is .2, or one stockout each 5 years).

The TAC associated with the policy Q = 12, R = 6 is $1619.53, or about 5.5% more than that associated with the optimum policy. The question might be raised: "Is a reduction in expected stockout frequency from 1 every 6 months to 1 every 5 years worth a 5.5% increase in total annual inventory costs?"

If the costs our wholesaler has chosen for COP, CPO, and SC are fair approximations of his actual costs, then clearly no increase in TAC from the minimum TAC is justified regardless of the reduction in stockout frequency, *so long as our objective is to minimize costs, and hence to maximize profit.*

This, of course, raises the question: "How sensitive is our wholesaler's inventory system to variations and hence to inaccuracies in estimating costs?"

Let us take stockout cost as an example.

Sensitivity to inaccuracies in estimating stockout cost for Item B. In Table 3-16 the optimum inventory policies associated with various per unit stockout costs are tabulated. Also shown are the minimum total annual inventory costs corresponding to the optimum policy in each case. In the next to last column are shown total costs which our wholesaler would actually incur if he based his inventory policy on a belief that per unit stockout cost was $40.00 *when in fact* stockout cost was as shown in the first column.

Obviously our wholesaler's system is not highly sensitive to inaccuracies in estimating stockout costs.

Table 3-16

Stockout cost (per unit)	Corresponding optimum inventory policy		Minimum total annual cost (based on optimum policy)	Total annual cost (if policy is based on estimated stockout cost of $40/unit)	Added inventory cost (attributable to ignorance of actual stockout cost)
	Q	R			
$20	14	3	$1,466	$1,473	0.5%
30	13	4	1,503	1,503	0.0
40	13	4	1,534	1,534	0.0
50	13	5	1,561	1,564	0.2
60	13	5	1,571	1,595	1.5
70	13	5	1,581	1,625	2.8

a practicable method for determining the optimum policy under uncertainty without quantity extras

If the costs of computation were zero, the method employed thus far to determine optimum policy would be satisfactory. But calculating costs associated with the full range of "reasonable" combinations of order quantities and reorder points would, in most real situations be impracticable.

What is required is a practicable shortcut. Let us use our wholesaler's model to develop a shortcut which, with modifications, can be used economically in real situations.

In what follows the mathematics gets a bit involved. We want to employ calculus, as we did in Chapter 2, to develop an EOQ model, but this time we want our EOQ model to incorporate the element of uncertainty. Understanding the *development* of the model is not crucial but understanding the restrictions in its use is crucial. In developing the model we will try to show why and in what way the model is restrictive.

Our general model under uncertainty, developed in the preceding pages, is:

$$TAC = [DPY/Q \times E(DDLT > R) \times SC] + [(Q/2 + R - DDLT) \times CPU \times COP] + [DPY/Q \times CPO]$$

Generally everything is assumed known in the expression above except Q, R and TAC. In our retailer's model everything was known except Q and TAC. In that model we employed calculus to find a model (the EOQ formula) which told us the value of Q which would cause TAC to be a minimum.

Our problem with the wholesaler's model above is that another unknown is present: R. To make the problem manageable we *assume* that the optimum order quantity is independent of the optimum reorder point. If we make this assumption we are asserting that we can determine the optimum reorder point, R, and then having R we can proceed to find the optimum order quantity, Q. This being the case we can assume that R is no longer an unknown in the model above, and therefore, as with our retailer's model, we are dealing only with the unknowns TAC & Q.

Now, having made this assumption we can use calculus to determine a general model (EOQ model) to tell us that value of Q which will cause TAC to be a minimum. As in our retailer's model we differentiate TAC, in the wholesaler's model above, with respect to Q, equate the result to zero and solve for Q:

$$\frac{dTAC}{dQ} = - DPY \times SC \times E(DDLT > R)/Q^2 + (\frac{1}{2} + R - DDLT) \times CPU \times COP - DPY \times CPO/Q^2$$

And now when: $dTAC/dQ = 0$,

$$Q = \sqrt{\frac{2DPY(CPO + E(DDLT > R) \times SC)}{COP \times CPU}} \qquad (3\text{-}2)$$

We know from the assumption we made when we developed model (3-2) above that if the optimum reorder point is known, we can get the optimum order quantity from (3-2). If our model is correct we should be able to get Q = 13 from (3-2), if we let R = 4, since we already know that our wholesaler's optimum policy is Q = 13, R = 4. Let us see:

$$Q = \sqrt{\frac{2 \times 365 \times (20 + .1091 \times 40)}{.20 \times 500}},$$
$$= 13 \text{ units.}$$

. . . and our expectation is confirmed.

By itself, however, model (3-2) is not very useful. We must know the optimum reorder point *before* we can use it to get the optimum order quantity.

In mathematical terms our problem is that we are really dealing with 2 unknowns but we have only one equation (3-2, our EOQ model above). If we had 2 equations in 2 unknowns we could solve them simultaneously for the 2 unknowns.

Let us see if further analysis of the inventory system will enable us to construct a second equation. We can do this if we address ourselves to the concept of the optimum probability of a stockout during lead time.

the optimum probability of meeting all demand during lead time and the optimum probability of a stockout during lead time

These two concepts are among the most important in inventory management theory. We can best understand them if we refer again to our wholesaler's model.

Suppose we know that the optimum order quantity is 13 units, but that we are uncertain about the optimum reorder point. To find this point we might select a very small value for R, check our total annual cost associated with $Q = 13$ and this small value for R; then we might increase our reorder point by 1 unit, check our total annual cost associated with $Q = 13$ and this slightly larger R; and continue doing this until we find that increasing R further does not yield savings in total annual cost.

Referring to Table 3-17 we find the following:

Q	R	TAC
13	2	$1911.66
13	3	1621.96
13	4	1534.07
13	5	1551.18

We would, of course, stop increasing R when we reached $R = 4$.

Notice that in this process of increasing R, a unit at a time, annual ordering cost does not change, but remains at $561.54. We expect this, since annual ordering cost depends on Q but not on R.

$$AOC = DPY/Q \times CPO$$

. . . and we're holding Q constant at $Q = 13$ units.

Q	R	AOC	AHC	ASC	TAC
13	2	$561.54	$650.00	$700.13	$1911.66
13	3	561.54	750.00	310.42	1621.96
13	4	561.54	850.00	122.53	1534.07
13	5	561.54	950.00	39.64	1551.18

As we increase R, a unit at a time, annual stockout cost is decreasing and annual holding cost is increasing:

When we increase R from 2 to 3 our annual stockout cost drops by $389.71 (700.13 — 310.42). Meantime, increasing R from 2 to 3 yields an increase in annual holding cost of only $100.00 (750.00 — 650.00).

Notice that when we increase R from 3 to 4 the saving in annual stockout cost is still greater than the increase in annual holding cost, but the margin is smaller:

Consequence of moving from R = 3 to R = 4:
Annual holding cost increase $100.00
Annual stockout cost decrease 187.89

It is apparent from the annual shortage column of Table 3-17 that when the reorder point is low (R is small) small incremental increases in R yield a substantial reduction in annual stockout, whereas when the reorder point is high (R is large) small incremental increases in R yield a very slight reduction in annual stockout.

Meantime, annual holding cost increases uniformly with unit increases in R.

Reasoning conversely, when R is already high, unit decreases in R yield very little added stockout hazard but yield substantial reduction in inventory. For example, if we reduce R from 9 to 8 units, expected annual shortage increases by less than 1/100 of a unit, and annual stockout cost increases by only $.34 (see Table 3-17). Meantime, however, by reducing R from 9 to 8 we reduce average inventory by 1 unit and therefore annual holding cost by $100.

It is because of this property of real inventory systems that we can make the statement, "*In any well managed inventory system, avoiding stockouts entirely is either impossible or economically undesirable.*"

Returning again to our wholesaler's problem, given the optimum order quantity, we should be willing to begin with a low reorder point and to increase it a *unit at a time* until savings in reduced stockouts are no longer sufficient to compensate for increases in holding cost. To be more specific, we would increase R, a unit at a time, until the annual stockout cost saving with each unit increase in R *is equal to* the added annual holding cost with each unit increase in R.

If we can express the last statement in the preceding paragraph in algebra we will have the second equation which we set out to find. To do this we reason as follows:

If we increase R by 1 unit the annual holding cost rises by the amount:

$$[Q/2 + (R + 1) - DDLT] \times CPU \times COP - [Q/2 + R - DDLT] \times CPU \times COP = CPU \times COP$$

Now, if we increase R by 1 unit what is the expected reduction in annual stockout cost? If *in any particular lead time period* we enjoy a stockout reduction it will be a reduction in stockout of 1 unit. We will experience this unit reduction in stockout during lead time if *more than* the original R is demanded; that is, if our current R = 3 and we increase it to R = 4, then we will enjoy a reduced stockout of 1 unit if more than 3 are demanded.

The *expected reduction* in stockout per lead time period associated with increasing R by one unit is therefore 1 x (the probability that *more than* R units will be demanded during lead time). Referring again to Table 3-9, the probability that demand during lead time will be greater than R, the cumulative probability, is the figure labeled $P(DDLT > R)$.

The expected reduction in units short per lead time period associated with increasing R by 1 is therefore:

$$1 \times P(DDLT > R)$$

Since we expect DPY/Q lead time periods per year the expected annual stockout reduction is:

$$1 \times P(DDLT > R) \times DPY/Q$$

The expected annual stockout saving associated with increasing R by 1 would be:

$$1 \times P(DDLT > R) \times DPY/Q \times SC$$

When this saving is just equal to the added annual holding cost associated with increasing R by 1 we have increased R enough. Our second equation, then, is:

$$1 \times P(DDLT > R) \times DPY/Q \times SC = CPU \times COP$$

If we solve this for $P(DDLT > R)$ we have:

$$P(DDLT > R) = CPU \times COP \times Q/(DPY \times SC)$$

The reorder point specified by this value of $P(DDLT > R)$ is our optimum reorder point, Thus, when $Q = 13$.

$$P(DDLT > R) = 500 \times .20 \times 13/(365 \times 40) = .088$$

Referring to Table 3-9 we find that this value of $P(DDLT > R)$ is closest to $R = 4$.

What, then, is the full meaning of the expression: $P(DDLT > R)$? With any reorder point there is an associated probability of a stockout during lead time. The optimum probability of a stockout during lead time, $P(DDLT > R)$, is the probability of a stockout associated with the optimum reorder point.

In our wholesaler's system, the probability of a stockout with $R = 2$ is .3470 x (see Table 3-9). This probabliity, which means an expected stockout in 34.7% of the lead time periods, is too high. With $R = 6$ the probability of a stockout is .0071, which means an expected stockout in .7% of the lead time periods. This is too low.

If our objective is to minimize inventory cost, then the optimum probability of a stockout, $P(DDLT > R)$, is .0738, meaning an expected stockout in 7.38% of the lead time periods.

If $P(DDLT > R)$ tells us the fraction of the lead time periods we should expect to get caught short with the optimum policy, then $1 - P(DDLT > R)$ should tell us the fraction of the lead time periods we should expect *not* to get caught short. Therefore, $1 - P(DDLT > R)$ is the optimum probability of meeting all demand during lead time.

While the optimum probability of a stockout during lead time may be difficult to visualize, "the optimum probability of meeting all demand during lead time" is somewhat more familiar.

We now have our 2 equations in 2 unknowns:

1. $$Q = \sqrt{\frac{2\,DPY(CPO + E(DDLT > R) \times SC)}{COP \times CPU}} \qquad (3\text{-}3)$$

2. $$P(DDLT > R) = CPU \times COP \times Q/(DPY \times SC) \qquad (3\text{-}4)[5]$$

---

[5]Where backordering is *not* permitted the form of this model changes to: $P(DDLT > R) = CPU \times COP \times Q/(DPY \times SC + CPU \times COP \times Q)$. More will be said about this form of (3-4) shortly.

Note: R is really the unknown in both E(DDLT > R) and P(DDLT > R), for once R is specified each of these expressions is specified.

Each of these 2 equations was developed by making an assumption. In developing equation (3-3) we assumed that R was known. In developing (3-4) we assumed Q was known.

The restriction imposed by these assumptions, when we move toward applying them in real inventory systems, is that we must use them interactively. An example will indicate how we can use equations (3-3) and (3-4) to determine the optimum inventory policy. We employ the following procedure:

1. *Assume a reorder point so large that a stockout is unimaginable.*
2. *Solve for Q, using (3-3).*
3. *Using this value for Q solve for P(DDLT > R) from (3-4).*
4. *Find the R associated with this value of P(DDLT > R) and use it to calculate a closer approximation of Q in equation (3-3).*
5. *Repeat steps 3 and 4 until further repetition yields no material change in Q and R.*

Generally a few iterations cause Q and R to "converge" to the optimum values of Q and R.

Referring to our wholesaler's system, step 1 obliges us to choose a reorder point so high that no stockout is possible. The expression E(DDLT > R), therefore, is zero, and equation (3-3) becomes:

$$Q = \sqrt{\frac{2 \times 365 \times 20}{.20 \times 500}} = 12$$

When Q = 12, equation (3-3) becomes:

$$P(DDLT > R) = 500 \times .20 \times 12 / (365 \times 40) = .089$$

From Table 3-9, the value of P (DDLT > R) closest to .089 is .0738, that corresponding to a reorder point of R= 4.

When R = 4, E(DDLT > R) =.1091 (from Table 3-9). With this superior approximation of E(DDLT > R) we are now equipped to find a closer approximation of Q from (3-3).

$$Q = \sqrt{\frac{2 \times 365 \ (500 + .1091 \times 40)}{.20 \times 500}} = 13 \text{ units}$$

Using this superior approximation of Q we employ (3-4) again to search for a better approximation of R:

$$P(DDLT > R) = 500 \text{ x } .20 \text{ x } 13/(365 \text{ x } 40) = .089$$

Again .089 is the cumulative probability of a stockout during lead time most closely associated with R = 4 (Table 3-9). By now we can conclude that further interations are unnecessary—they would not yield values for Q and R significantly different from those we already have.

While the procedure seems cumbersome, usually only a few iterations are required to determine the optimum combination of Q and R. Where quantity extras are quoted by suppliers the interaction between Q and R, using the models (3-3) and (3-4), is even less— further simplifying the calculations.

Before addressing ourselves to the implications of the introduction of quantity extras, let us observe a final property of our models (3-3) and (3-4).

Solving for the optimum *combination* of Q and R requires the iterative process exemplified above. Given a particular order quantity, however, (3-4) can be employed to determine the best reorder point. Similarly, given a reorder point (3-3) can be employed to determine the best order quantity.

Assume, for example, that our wholesaler cannot order fewer than 17 units with each order placed. From (3-4) we have:

$$P(DDLT > R) = 500 \text{ x } .20 \text{ x } 17/(365 \text{ x } 40) = .116$$

From Table 3-9 we find that his best reorder point, that reorder point for which $P(DDLT > R)$ is nearest .116, is 3. A recheck of the TAC figures in Table 3-17 confirms again that for Q = 17 a reorder point of R = 3 is best.

Assume that our wholesaler's stock level has passed through his optimum reorder point to R = 2. When R = 2 E(DDLT > R) = .2764 from (3-3) we have:

$$Q = \sqrt{\frac{2 \text{ x } 365(20 + .2764 \text{ x } 40)}{.20 \text{ x } 500}} = 12 \text{ units}$$

A recheck of the TAC figures in Table 3-17 confirms again that for R = 2 an order quantity Q = 12 is best.

Table 3-17

With Expected Demand Per Year = 365 Units, At Delivered Cost of $500 Per Unit
Annual Materials Cost = $182,500

WITH REORDER POINT SET AT 2 UNITS

	AVERAGE INVENTORY	ANNUAL SHORTAGE	AHC	AOC	ASC	TAC	TAC INCLUDING MATERIALS COST
WHEN Q = 2 UNITS	1.0	113.8	100.00	3650.00	4550.82	8300.82	190800.82
WHEN Q = 3 UNITS	1.5	75.8	150.00	2433.33	3033.88	5617.21	188117.21
WHEN Q = 4 UNITS	2.0	56.9	200.00	1825.00	2275.41	4300.41	186800.41
WHEN Q = 5 UNITS	2.5	45.5	250.00	1460.00	1820.33	3530.33	186030.33
WHEN Q = 6 UNITS	3.0	37.9	300.00	1216.67	1516.94	3033.61	185533.61
WHEN Q = 7 UNITS	3.5	32.5	350.00	1042.86	1300.23	2693.09	185193.09
WHEN Q = 8 UNITS	4.0	28.4	400.00	912.50	1137.71	2450.21	184950.21
WHEN Q = 9 UNITS	4.5	25.3	450.00	811.11	1011.29	2272.40	184772.40
WHEN Q = 10 UNITS	5.0	22.8	500.00	730.00	910.16	2140.16	184640.16
WHEN Q = 11 UNITS	5.5	20.7	550.00	663.64	827.42	2041.06	184541.06
WHEN Q = 12 UNITS	6.0	19.0	600.00	608.33	758.47	1966.80	184466.80
WHEN Q = 13 UNITS	6.5	17.5	650.00	561.54	700.13	1911.66	184411.66
WHEN Q = 14 UNITS	7.0	16.3	700.00	521.43	650.12	1871.55	184371.55
WHEN Q = 15 UNITS	7.5	15.2	750.00	486.67	606.78	1843.44	184343.44
WHEN Q = 16 UNITS	8.0	14.2	800.00	456.25	568.85	1825.10	184325.10
WHEN Q = 17 UNITS	8.5	13.4	850.00	429.41	535.39	1814.80	184314.80
WHEN Q = 18 UNITS	9.0	12.6	900.00	405.56	505.65	1811.20	184311.20
WHEN Q = 19 UNITS	9.5	12.0	950.00	384.21	479.03	1813.24	184313.24
WHEN Q = 20 UNITS	10.0	11.4	1000.00	365.00	455.08	1820.08	184320.08
WHEN Q = 21 UNITS	10.5	10.8	1050.00	347.62	433.41	1831.03	184331.03
WHEN Q = 22 UNITS	11.0	10.3	1100.00	331.82	413.71	1845.53	184345.53
WHEN Q = 23 UNITS	11.5	9.9	1150.00	317.39	395.72	1863.11	184363.11
WHEN Q = 24 UNITS	12.0	9.5	1200.00	304.17	379.24	1883.40	184383.40
WHEN Q = 25 UNITS	12.5	9.1	1250.00	292.00	364.07	1906.07	184406.07
WHEN Q = 26 UNITS	13.0	8.8	1300.00	280.77	350.06	1930.83	184430.83
WHEN Q = 27 UNITS	13.5	8.4	1350.00	270.37	337.10	1957.47	184457.47
WHEN Q = 28 UNITS	14.0	8.1	1400.00	260.71	325.06	1985.77	184485.77
WHEN Q = 29 UNITS	14.5	7.8	1450.00	251.72	313.85	2015.57	184515.57

(Continued)

Table 3-17 (Continued)

WITH REORDER POINT SET AT 3 UNITS

	AVERAGE INVENTORY	ANNUAL SHORTAGE	AHC	AOC	ASC	TAC	TAC INCLUDING MATERIALS COST
WHEN Q = 2 UNITS	2.0	50.4	200.00	3650.00	2017.72	5867.72	188367.72
WHEN Q = 3 UNITS	2.5	33.6	250.00	2433.33	1345.15	4028.48	186528.48
WHEN Q = 4 UNITS	3.0	25.2	300.00	1825.00	1008.86	3133.86	185633.86
WHEN Q = 5 UNITS	3.5	20.2	350.00	1460.00	807.09	2617.09	185117.09
WHEN Q = 6 UNITS	4.0	16.8	400.00	1216.67	672.57	2289.24	184789.24
WHEN Q = 7 UNITS	4.5	14.4	450.00	1042.86	576.49	2069.35	184569.35
WHEN Q = 8 UNITS	5.0	12.6	500.00	912.50	504.43	1916.93	184416.93
WHEN Q = 9 UNITS	5.5	11.2	550.00	811.11	448.38	1809.49	184309.49
WHEN Q = 10 UNITS	6.0	10.1	600.00	730.00	403.54	1733.54	184233.54
WHEN Q = 11 UNITS	6.5	9.2	650.00	663.64	366.86	1680.49	184180.49
WHEN Q = 12 UNITS	7.0	8.4	700.00	608.33	336.29	1644.62	184144.62
WHEN Q = 13 UNITS	7.5	7.8	750.00	561.54	310.42	1621.96	184121.96
WHEN Q = 14 UNITS	8.0	7.2	800.00	521.43	288.25	1609.67	184109.67
WHEN Q = 15 UNITS	8.5	6.7	850.00	486.67	269.03	1605.70	184105.70
WHEN Q = 16 UNITS	9.0	6.3	900.00	456.25	252.22	1608.47	184108.47
WHEN Q = 17 UNITS	9.5	5.9	950.00	429.41	237.38	1616.79	184116.79
WHEN Q = 18 UNITS	10.0	5.6	1000.00	405.56	224.19	1629.75	184129.75
WHEN Q = 19 UNITS	10.5	5.3	1050.00	384.21	212.39	1646.60	184146.60
WHEN Q = 20 UNITS	11.0	5.0	1100.00	365.00	201.77	1666.77	184166.77
WHEN Q = 21 UNITS	11.5	4.8	1150.00	347.62	192.16	1689.78	184189.78
WHEN Q = 22 UNITS	12.0	4.6	1200.00	331.82	183.43	1715.25	184215.25
WHEN Q = 23 UNITS	12.5	4.4	1250.00	317.39	175.45	1742.85	184242.85
WHEN Q = 24 UNITS	13.0	4.2	1300.00	304.17	168.14	1772.31	184272.31
WHEN Q = 25 UNITS	13.5	4.0	1350.00	292.00	161.42	1803.42	184303.42
WHEN Q = 26 UNITS	14.0	3.9	1400.00	280.77	155.21	1835.98	184335.98
WHEN Q = 27 UNITS	14.5	3.7	1450.00	270.37	149.46	1869.83	184369.83
WHEN Q = 28 UNITS	15.0	3.6	1500.00	260.71	144.12	1904.84	184404.84
WHEN Q = 29 UNITS	15.5	3.5	1550.00	251.72	139.15	1940.88	184440.88

(Continued)

Table 3-17 (Continued)

WITH REORDER POINT SET AT 4 UNITS

	AVERAGE INVENTORY	ANNUAL SHORTAGE	AHC	AOC	ASC	TAC	TAC INCLUDING MATERIALS COST
WHEN Q = 2 UNITS	3.0	19.9	300.00	3650.00	796.43	4746.43	187246.43
WHEN Q = 3 UNITS	3.5	13.3	350.00	2433.33	530.95	3314.29	185814.29
WHEN Q = 4 UNITS	4.0	10.0	400.00	1825.00	398.21	2623.22	185123.22
WHEN Q = 5 UNITS	4.5	8.0	450.00	1460.00	318.57	2228.57	184728.57
WHEN Q = 6 UNITS	5.0	6.6	500.00	1216.67	265.48	1982.14	184482.14
WHEN Q = 7 UNITS	5.5	5.7	550.00	1042.86	227.55	1820.41	184320.41
WHEN Q = 8 UNITS	6.0	5.0	600.00	912.50	199.11	1711.61	184211.61
WHEN Q = 9 UNITS	6.5	4.4	650.00	811.11	176.98	1638.10	184138.10
WHEN Q = 10 UNITS	7.0	4.0	700.00	730.00	159.29	1589.20	184089.29
WHEN Q = 11 UNITS	7.5	3.6	750.00	663.64	144.81	1558.44	184058.44
WHEN Q = 12 UNITS	8.0	3.3	800.00	608.33	132.74	1541.07	184041.07
WHEN Q = 13 UNITS	8.5	3.1	850.00	561.54	122.53	1534.07	184034.07
WHEN Q = 14 UNITS	9.0	2.8	900.00	521.43	113.78	1535.20	184035.20
WHEN Q = 15 UNITS	9.5	2.7	950.00	486.67	106.19	1542.86	184042.86
WHEN Q = 16 UNITS	10.0	2.5	1000.00	456.25	99.55	1555.80	184055.80
WHEN Q = 17 UNITS	10.5	2.3	1050.00	429.41	93.70	1573.11	184073.11
WHEN Q = 18 UNITS	11.0	2.2	1100.00	405.56	88.49	1594.05	184094.05
WHEN Q = 19 UNITS	11.5	2.1	1150.00	384.21	83.83	1618.05	184118.05
WHEN Q = 20 UNITS	12.0	2.0	1200.00	365.00	79.64	1644.64	184144.64
WHEN Q = 21 UNITS	12.5	1.9	1250.00	347.62	75.85	1673.47	184173.47
WHEN Q = 22 UNITS	13.0	1.8	1300.00	331.82	72.40	1704.22	184204.22
WHEN Q = 23 UNITS	13.5	1.7	1350.00	317.39	69.25	1736.65	184236.65
WHEN Q = 24 UNITS	14.0	1.7	1400.00	304.17	66.37	1770.54	184270.54
WHEN Q = 25 UNITS	14.5	1.6	1450.00	292.00	63.71	1805.71	184305.71
WHEN Q = 26 UNITS	15.0	1.5	1500.00	280.77	61.26	1842.03	184342.03
WHEN Q = 27 UNITS	15.5	1.5	1550.00	270.37	58.99	1879.37	184379.37
WHEN Q = 28 UNITS	16.0	1.4	1600.00	260.71	56.89	1917.60	184417.60
WHEN Q = 29 UNITS	16.5	1.4	1650.00	251.72	54.93	1956.65	184456.65

(Continued)

Table 3-17 (Continued)

WITH REORDER POINT SET AT 5 UNITS

	AVERAGE INVENTORY	ANNUAL SHORTAGE	AHC	AOC	ASC	TAC	TAC INCLUDING MATERIALS COST
WHEN Q = 2 UNITS	4.0	6.4	400.00	3650.00	257.69	4307.69	186807.69
WHEN Q = 3 UNITS	4.5	4.3	450.00	2433.33	171.79	3055.13	185555.13
WHEN Q = 4 UNITS	5.0	3.2	500.00	1825.00	128.85	2453.85	184953.85
WHEN Q = 5 UNITS	5.5	2.6	550.00	1460.00	103.08	2113.08	184613.08
WHEN Q = 6 UNITS	6.0	2.1	600.00	1216.67	85.90	1902.56	184402.56
WHEN Q = 7 UNITS	6.5	1.8	650.00	1042.86	73.63	1766.48	184266.48
WHEN Q = 8 UNITS	7.0	1.6	700.00	912.50	64.42	1676.92	184176.92
WHEN Q = 9 UNITS	7.5	1.4	750.00	811.11	57.26	1618.38	184118.38
WHEN Q = 10 UNITS	8.0	1.3	800.00	730.00	51.54	1581.54	184081.54
WHEN Q = 11 UNITS	8.5	1.2	850.00	663.64	46.85	1560.49	184060.49
WHEN Q = 12 UNITS	9.0	1.1	900.00	608.33	42.95	1551.28	184051.28
WHEN Q = 13 UNITS	9.5	1.0	950.00	561.54	39.64	1551.18	184051.18
WHEN Q = 14 UNITS	10.0	.9	1000.00	521.43	36.81	1558.24	184058.24
WHEN Q = 15 UNITS	10.5	.9	1050.00	486.67	34.36	1571.03	184071.03
WHEN Q = 16 UNITS	11.0	.8	1100.00	456.25	32.21	1588.46	184088.46
WHEN Q = 17 UNITS	11.5	.8	1150.00	429.41	30.32	1609.73	184109.73
WHEN Q = 18 UNITS	12.0	.7	1200.00	405.56	28.63	1634.19	184134.19
WHEN Q = 19 UNITS	12.5	.7	1250.00	384.21	27.13	1661.34	184161.34
WHEN Q = 20 UNITS	13.0	.6	1300.00	365.00	25.77	1690.77	184190.77
WHEN Q = 21 UNITS	13.5	.6	1350.00	347.62	24.54	1722.16	184222.16
WHEN Q = 22 UNITS	14.0	.6	1400.00	331.82	23.43	1755.24	184255.24
WHEN Q = 23 UNITS	14.5	.6	1450.00	317.39	22.41	1789.80	184289.80
WHEN Q = 24 UNITS	15.0	.5	1500.00	304.17	21.47	1825.64	184325.64
WHEN Q = 25 UNITS	15.5	.5	1550.00	292.00	20.62	1862.62	184367.62
WHEN Q = 26 UNITS	16.0	.5	1600.00	280.77	19.82	1900.59	184400.59
WHEN Q = 27 UNITS	16.5	.5	1650.00	270.37	19.09	1939.46	184439.46
WHEN Q = 28 UNITS	17.0	.5	1700.00	260.71	18.41	1979.12	184479.12
WHEN Q = 29 UNITS	17.5	.4	1750.00	251.72	17.77	2019.50	184519.50

(Continued)

Table 3-17 (Continued)

WITH REORDER POINT SET AT 6 UNITS

	AVERAGE INVENTORY	ANNUAL SHORTAGE	AHC	AOC	ASC	TAC	TAC INCLUDING MATERIALS COST
WHEN Q = 2 UNITS	5.0	1.7	500.00	3650.00	67.16	4217.16	186717.16
WHEN Q = 3 UNITS	5.5	1.1	550.00	2433.33	44.77	3028.11	185528.11
WHEN Q = 4 UNITS	6.0	.8	600.00	1825.00	33.58	2458.58	184958.58
WHEN Q = 5 UNITS	6.5	.7	650.00	1460.00	26.86	2136.86	184636.86
WHEN Q = 6 UNITS	7.0	.6	700.00	1216.67	22.39	1939.05	184439.05
WHEN Q = 7 UNITS	7.5	.5	750.00	1042.86	19.19	1812.05	184312.05
WHEN Q = 8 UNITS	8.0	.4	800.00	912.50	16.79	1729.29	184229.29
WHEN Q = 9 UNITS	8.5	.4	850.00	811.11	14.92	1676.04	184176.04
WHEN Q = 10 UNITS	9.0	.3	900.00	730.00	13.43	1643.43	184143.43
WHEN Q = 11 UNITS	9.5	.3	950.00	663.64	12.21	1625.85	184125.85
WHEN Q = 12 UNITS	10.0	.3	1000.00	608.33	11.19	1619.53	184119.53
WHEN Q = 13 UNITS	10.5	.3	1050.00	561.54	10.33	1621.87	184121.87
WHEN Q = 14 UNITS	11.0	.2	1100.00	521.43	9.59	1631.02	184131.02
WHEN Q = 15 UNITS	11.5	.2	1150.00	486.67	8.95	1645.62	184145.62
WHEN Q = 16 UNITS	12.0	.2	1200.00	456.25	8.40	1664.65	184164.65
WHEN Q = 17 UNITS	12.5	.2	1250.00	429.41	7.90	1687.31	184187.31
WHEN Q = 18 UNITS	13.0	.2	1300.00	405.56	7.46	1713.02	184213.02
WHEN Q = 19 UNITS	13.5	.2	1350.00	384.21	7.07	1741.28	184241.28
WHEN Q = 20 UNITS	14.0	.2	1400.00	365.00	6.72	1771.72	184271.72
WHEN Q = 21 UNITS	14.5	.2	1450.00	347.62	6.40	1804.02	184304.02
WHEN Q = 22 UNITS	15.0	.2	1500.00	331.82	6.11	1837.92	184337.92
WHEN Q = 23 UNITS	15.5	.1	1550.00	317.39	5.84	1873.23	184373.23
WHEN Q = 24 UNITS	16.0	.1	1600.00	304.17	5.60	1909.76	184409.76
WHEN Q = 25 UNITS	16.5	.1	1650.00	292.00	5.37	1947.37	184447.37
WHEN Q = 26 UNITS	17.0	.1	1700.00	280.77	5.17	1985.94	184485.94
WHEN Q = 27 UNITS	17.5	.1	1750.00	270.37	4.97	2025.35	184525.35
WHEN Q = 28 UNITS	18.0	.1	1800.00	260.71	4.80	2065.51	184565.51
WHEN Q = 29 UNITS	18.5	.1	1850.00	251.72	4.63	2106.36	184606.36

(Continued)

Table 3-17 (Continued)

WITH REORDER POINT SET AT 7 UNITS

	AVERAGE INVENTORY	ANNUAL SHORTAGE	AHC	AOC	ASC	TAC	TAC INCLUDING MATERIALS COST
WHEN Q = 2 UNITS	6.0	.4	600.00	3650.00	15.33	4265.33	186765.33
WHEN Q = 3 UNITS	6.5	.3	650.00	2433.33	10.22	3093.55	185593.55
WHEN Q = 4 UNITS	7.0	.2	700.00	1825.00	7.66	2532.67	185032.67
WHEN Q = 5 UNITS	7.5	.2	750.00	1460.00	6.13	2216.13	184716.13
WHEN Q = 6 UNITS	8.0	.1	800.00	1216.67	5.11	2021.78	184521.78
WHEN Q = 7 UNITS	8.5	.1	850.00	1042.86	4.38	1897.24	184397.24
WHEN Q = 8 UNITS	9.0	.1	900.00	912.50	3.83	1816.33	184316.33
WHEN Q = 9 UNITS	9.5	.1	950.00	811.11	3.41	1764.52	184264.52
WHEN Q = 10 UNITS	10.0	.1	1000.00	730.00	3.07	1733.07	184233.07
WHEN Q = 11 UNITS	10.5	.1	1050.00	663.64	2.79	1716.42	184216.42
WHEN Q = 12 UNITS	11.0	.1	1100.00	608.33	2.55	1710.89	184210.89
WHEN Q = 13 UNITS	11.5	.1	1150.00	561.54	2.36	1713.90	184213.90
WHEN Q = 14 UNITS	12.0	.1	1200.00	521.43	2.19	1723.62	184223.62
WHEN Q = 15 UNITS	12.5	.1	1250.00	486.67	2.04	1738.71	184238.71
WHEN Q = 16 UNITS	13.0	.0	1300.00	456.25	1.92	1758.17	184258.17
WHEN Q = 17 UNITS	13.5	.0	1350.00	429.41	1.80	1781.22	184281.22
WHEN Q = 18 UNITS	14.0	.0	1400.00	405.56	1.70	1807.26	184307.26
WHEN Q = 19 UNITS	14.5	.0	1450.00	384.21	1.61	1835.82	184335.82
WHEN Q = 20 UNITS	15.0	.0	1500.00	365.00	1.53	1866.53	184366.53
WHEN Q = 21 UNITS	15.5	.0	1550.00	347.62	1.46	1899.08	184399.08
WHEN Q = 22 UNITS	16.0	.0	1600.00	331.82	1.39	1933.21	184433.21
WHEN Q = 23 UNITS	16.5	.0	1650.00	317.39	1.33	1968.72	184468.72
WHEN Q = 24 UNITS	17.0	.0	1700.00	304.17	1.28	2005.44	184505.44
WHEN Q = 25 UNITS	17.5	.0	1750.00	292.00	1.23	2043.23	184543.23
WHEN Q = 26 UNITS	18.0	.0	1800.00	280.77	1.18	2081.95	184581.95
WHEN Q = 27 UNITS	18.5	.0	1850.00	270.37	1.14	2121.51	184621.51
WHEN Q = 28 UNITS	19.0	.0	1900.00	260.71	1.09	2161.81	184661.81
WHEN Q = 29 UNITS	19.5	.0	1950.00	251.72	1.06	2202.78	184702.78

(Continued)

Table 3-17   (Continued)

WITH REORDER POINT SET AT 8 UNITS

WHEN Q = UNITS	AVERAGE INVENTORY	ANNUAL SHORTAGE	AHC	AOC	ASC	TAC	TAC INCLUDING MATERIALS COST
WHEN Q = 2 UNITS	7.0	.1	700.00	3650.00	2.19	4352.19	186852.19
WHEN Q = 3 UNITS	7.5	.0	750.00	2433.33	1.46	3184.79	185684.79
WHEN Q = 4 UNITS	8.0	.0	800.00	1825.00	1.09	2626.10	185126.10
WHEN Q = 5 UNITS	8.5	.0	850.00	1460.00	.88	2310.88	184810.88
WHEN Q = 6 UNITS	9.0	.0	900.00	1216.67	.73	2117.40	184617.40
WHEN Q = 7 UNITS	9.5	.0	950.00	1042.86	.63	1993.48	184493.48
WHEN Q = 8 UNITS	10.0	.0	1000.00	912.50	.55	1913.05	184413.05
WHEN Q = 9 UNITS	10.5	.0	1050.00	811.11	.49	1861.60	184361.60
WHEN Q = 10 UNITS	11.0	.0	1100.00	730.00	.44	1830.44	184330.44
WHEN Q = 11 UNITS	11.5	.0	1150.00	663.64	.40	1814.03	184314.03
WHEN Q = 12 UNITS	12.0	.0	1200.00	608.33	.36	1808.70	184308.70
WHEN Q = 13 UNITS	12.5	.0	1250.00	561.54	.34	1811.88	184311.88
WHEN Q = 14 UNITS	13.0	.0	1300.00	521.43	.31	1821.74	184321.74
WHEN Q = 15 UNITS	13.5	.0	1350.00	486.67	.29	1836.96	184336.96
WHEN Q = 16 UNITS	14.0	.0	1400.00	456.25	.27	1856.52	184356.52
WHEN Q = 17 UNITS	14.5	.0	1450.00	429.41	.26	1879.67	184379.67
WHEN Q = 18 UNITS	15.0	.0	1500.00	405.56	.24	1905.80	184405.80
WHEN Q = 19 UNITS	15.5	.0	1550.00	384.21	.23	1934.44	184434.44
WHEN Q = 20 UNITS	16.0	.0	1600.00	365.00	.22	1965.22	184465.22
WHEN Q = 21 UNITS	16.5	.0	1650.00	347.62	.21	1997.83	184497.83
WHEN Q = 22 UNITS	17.0	.0	1700.00	331.82	.20	2032.02	184532.02
WHEN Q = 23 UNITS	17.5	.0	1750.00	317.39	.19	2067.58	184567.58
WHEN Q = 24 UNITS	18.0	.0	1800.00	304.17	.18	2104.35	184604.35
WHEN Q = 25 UNITS	18.5	.0	1850.00	292.00	.18	2142.18	184642.18
WHEN Q = 26 UNITS	19.0	.0	1900.00	280.77	.17	2180.94	184680.94
WHEN Q = 27 UNITS	19.5	.0	1950.00	270.37	.16	2220.53	184720.53
WHEN Q = 28 UNITS	20.0	.0	2000.00	260.71	.16	2260.87	184760.87
WHEN Q = 29 UNITS	20.5	.0	2050.00	251.72	.15	2301.88	184801.88

4 a simple inventory problem under uncertainty with quantity extras

FOR ADDED EMPHASIS LET US REPEAT again the three specications by which the optimum inventory policy can be expressed:

1. *The optimum reorder point, R*
2. *The optimum order quantity, Q*
3. *The optimum frequency of policy review*

And, again, these three specifications result from an analysis of:

1. *Annual holding cost, AHC*
2. *Annual ordering cost, AOC*
3. *Annual stockout cost, ASC*
4. *Annual materials cost, AMC*
5. *The rate of change of the preceding 4, and the rate of change of demand and lead time*

In this chapter we will add quantity extras, and therefore factor 4 enters our analysis, but we will continue to assume that while demand and lead time are uncertain, they are characterized by probability distributions which are not expected to change. Factor 5 therefore is eliminated from our analysis and we are not concerned with the third *specification* above.

the effect of quantity extras

Let us continue to use our wholesaler's model of Chapter 3 for illustrative purposes. Let us assume, however, that our wholesaler's suppliers quote the following delivered price schedule for Item B:

Order quantity (units)	Cost/unit
01 thru 29	$500
30 thru 55	495
56 thru 83	493
over 83	492

The suppliers' base price is, therefore, $492 per unit with the following quantity extras:

Order quantity (units)	Quantity extra per unit)
56 thru 83	$1
30 thru 55	3
less than 30	8

We found in Chapter 3 that at an unvarying cost per unit for Item B of $500, the optimum policy was Q = 13, R = 4. With the introduction of the quantity extras schedule above we must now ask ourselves whether it might not pay to order 30 units of Item B and exploit a per unit materials cost saving of $5.

The problem with which we are confronted would *appear* to be: Would the reduction in annual materials cost associated with ordering in lots of 30 rather than 13 be sufficient to compensate for the added annual holding cost?"

This is not the complete problem however. The optimum reorder point and the optimum order quantity, as we have seen, are interdependent. If we increase Q to 30 our optimum reorder point will change. It seems, therefore, that we cannot test the superiority of a Q of 30 simply by comparing annual materials cost saving with increased annual holding cost.

To test whether we can ignore the effect on R of increasing Q, to take advantage of a price break, let us examine the costs associated with a variety of combinations of Q and R in each of the price ranges specified by our quantity extra schedule.

In Table 4-1, at the end of this chapter, we have operating costs associated with a delivered cost of CPU = $495, as Q varies from 30 through 55 and as R varies from 2 through 8. In Table 4-2 CPU = $493 and Q varies from 56 through 83 while R varies from 2 through 8. Finally in Table 4-3 CPU = $492 and Q varies from 84 through 110 while R varies from 2 through 8.

In Tables 3-17 (Chapter 3), 4-1, 4-2 and 4-3 we have all the "feasible" policies and their associated costs. In comparing policies we must now focus our attention on the *final* column of these tables which tells us total annual cost *including material cost*.

Total annual cost including material cost associated with our optimum policy of Q= 13, R = 4, when cost per unit is constant at $500, is $184,034.07 (Table 3-17). Referring to the final column of Table 4-1 we see that total annual cost including materials cost associated with an order quantity of Q = 30 is less than $184,034.07.

Placing larger orders to take advantage of a price break is clearly advantageous to our wholesaler.

If we look more closely at the various sets of data in Table 4-1 we see that regardless of what reorder point we employ an order quantity of Q = 30 is best.

The best *reorder point* for a Q of 30, however, proves to be R= 3 units. We have already observed the interdependence of Q and R so this should not surprise us. By increasing Q from 13 to 30 we more than halve the expected number of lead time periods per year and hence the number of stockout opportunities. With the number of stockouts thus reduced, it becomes advantageous to "trade off" a slightly increased stockout during lead time for reduced average inventory by reducing R from 4 to 3 units.

Would a further increase in Q, specifically a move to the next price break (to Q = 56), be advantageous? Referring to Tables 4-2 and 4-3, it is apparent that an order quantity of Q = 56 would be better than an order quantity of Q = 13, but not superior to an order quantity of Q = 30.

The optimum policy for Item B with Quantity Extras. It is apparent, therefore, that our wholesaler's optimum policy is:

"When the stock level in Item B drops to 3 units, reorder 30 units."

With this policy the sum of the following costs will be minimized:

1. *Annual holding cost, AHC*
2. *Annual ordering cost, AOC*
3. *Annual stockout cost, ASC*
4. *Annual materials cost, AMC*

a practicable method for determining the optimum policy under uncertainty with quantity extras

As we observed in Chapter 3, the cost of computation is not zero. It is not practicable at this stage of the arts to determine optimum inventory policy by calculating costs associated with all reasonable, feasible policies. Let us see if we can use the two models we developed in Chapter 3, (3-3) and (3-4), to determine the optimum policy with quantity extras.

Let us assume that our wholesaler has no notion whatever about the optimum policy for Item B. He might then begin by assuming that his optimum policy will involve an order quantity which obliges him to pay the highest per unit price for Item B; that is, the largest of the quantity extras.

In using model (3-3), therefore, he will employ a cost per unit CPU = $500. Following our iterative procedure he will assume an initial reorder point so high that no stockout will occur, and calculate an initial value for Q as follows:

$$Q = \sqrt{\frac{2 \text{ x } 365 \text{ x } 20}{.20 \text{ x } 500}} = 12 \text{ units}$$

Next, using this initial value for Q he will employ model (3-4) to get an initial approximation for R.

P(DDLT > R) = 5000 x .20 x 12/(365 x 40) = .082

This value for the probability of a stockout during lead time corresponds most closely to R = 4 (Table 3-9). When R = 4, E(DDLT > R) = .1091. Using this value for E(DDLT > R) we search for a better approximation of Q, using (3-3):

$$Q = \sqrt{\frac{2 \text{ x } 365 \ (20 \text{ x } .1091 \text{ x } 40)}{.20 \text{ x } 500}} = 13 \text{ units}$$

. . . . as we expected.

Our wholesaler should now employ models (3-3) and (3-4) to check the potential advantage in moving into the first price break, Q = 30.

The cost per unit associated with Q = 30 is $495. Our wholesaler then must employ CPU = $495 in his next use of (3-3) and (3-4). As before, he begins again by assuming initially a reorder point so high that a stockout will not occur and calculates an initial approximation for Q:

$$Q = \sqrt{\frac{2 \text{ x } 365 \text{ x } 20}{.20 \text{ x } 495}} = 12 \text{ units}$$

An order quantity of 12 units associated with a cost per unit of $495 is not feasible. However, an order quantity of 30 associated with a cost per unit of $495 *is* feasible. Therefore, let us assume CPU = $495 and Q = 30 and employ model (3-4) to determine the optimum reorder point.

P(DDLT > R) = 495 x .20 x 30/(365 x 40) = .203

This value for the cumulative probability is closest to R = 3, confirming our previous conclusion (based on a search of Table 4-1) that with Q = 30 the optimum reorder point is R = 3 units.

What do we have thus far? We have discovered only that if we intend to order in lots of Q = 30, then our best reorder point is R = 3. Models (3-3) and (3-4) have *not* helped us determine if the total annual cost including materials cost at Q = 30, R = 3 and CPU = $495 is better than Q = 13, R = 4 and CPU = $500.

Let us try another strategy. Models (3-3) and (3-4) have told us that if CPU = $500 the best policy is Q = 13 and R = 4. Let us use the general total annual cost model which we developed in Chapter 3, adding to it the cost of materials (DPY x CPU), to determine the total cost associated with the optimum policy at CPU = $500, and also the total cost associated with CPU = $495, Q = 30 and R = 3.[1]

$$\text{TACIM} = [\text{DPY}/Q \text{ x } E(\text{DDLT} > R) \text{ x SC}] + [(Q/2 + R-\text{DDLT}) \text{ x CPU x COP}] + [\text{DPY}/Q \text{ x CPO}] + [\text{DPY x CPU}]$$

$$(4\text{-}1)$$

With CPU = $500, Q = 13 and R = 4, model (4-1) becomes:
$$\text{TACIM} = [365/13 \text{ x } .1091 \text{ x } 40] + [(13/2 + 4\text{-}2) \text{ x } 500 \text{ x } .20] + [365/13 \text{ x } 20] + [365 \text{ x } 500] = \$184,034.07$$

With CPU = \$495, Q = 30 and R = 3, model (4-1) becomes:
TACIM = [365/30 x .2764 x 40] + [(30/2 + 3-2) x 495 x .20]
    + [365/30 x 20] + [365 x 495] = \$182,636.85

Clearly total cost is less with CPU = \$495, Q = 30 and R = 3.

Two questions must occur to our wholesaler:

1. *Might not a move to some other order quantity in the range
   Q = 30 through Q = 55 be more advantageous yet?*
2. *Would it further pay to move on to the NEXT price break?*

Let us address ourselves to question 1 first. By now we have become aware of the nature of the interaction between Q and R. While
they are interdependent *large changes in Q yield relatively small
changes in R* from:

$$P(DDLT > R) = CPU \ x \ COP \ x \ Q/(DPY \ x \ SC)$$

Meantime, small changes in R yield rather small changes in Q
from:

$$Q = \sqrt{\frac{2 \ x \ DPY \ (CPO + E(DDLT > R) \ x \ SC)}{COP \ x \ CPU}}$$

Let us assume, therefore, that we are going to adopt R = 4 as our
reorder point and see what happens to TACIM as we let Q vary
through the 2 price breaks from Q = 2 to Q = 100 (see Figure 4-1).

The segments of the curve of Figure 4-1 which are drawn with
solid lines represent our "feasible" policies; that is, points on each
segment represent total annual costs including materials cost based
on per unit costs for Item B which correspond to the order quantity
ranges quoted in the quantity extra schedule.

It is apparent that *any* order quantity in the range 30 through 55
(corresponding to CPU = \$495) is better than the optimum order
quantity (Q = 13) associated with CPU = \$500. It is also apparent
that some order quantities in the range 56 through 83 are better than
the optimum quantity associated with CPU = \$500.

The best order quantities in the ranges corresponding to costs
per unit of \$495 and \$493 are obviously at the price breaks. That is to
say, our total cost curve segments associated with the price breaks are
not U-shaped but curve upward toward the right, so that the minimum
points on these segments are the left-most points.

The reason for this is clear: the extremely high cost associated with extremely small order quantities is largely ordering cost. As we observed in Chapter 2 when we increase the order quantity by small increments, beginning with a very *low* order quantity, we enjoy large reductions in annual ordering cost. As we increase the order quantity by small increments beginning with a high order quantity, however, we do not reduce annual ordering cost significantly. Meantime, however, incremental increases in the order quantity yield uniform increases in annual holding cost.

As we increase Q, then, we soon reach a point where further increases in Q do not yield ordering cost savings adequate to compensate for the increased holding cost. This point occurs where the annual ordering cost equals the annual holding cost (at this point these two curves cross—see Figure 2-3).

This brings us to a very important principle:

In real inventory systems, *once we've passed the point where annual ordering cost equals annual holding cost* the slope of our total annual cost curve is always upward toward the right. This means that if there is an advantage in ordering in quantities larger than the order quantity corresponding to the point where these two curves cross, *the best order quantity will always be at a price break.*[2]

In answer to the first of the two questions we posed above, therefore, we can state that having discovered, through the use of models (3-3) and (3-4), that there *is* an optimum policy associated with a particular cost per unit for Item B, any superior policy will be at a price break.

To answer the second of the questions posed, therefore, we simply employ model (4-1) using the cost per unit in the next price catagory and the order quantity at the price break; that is, CPU = $495, Q = 30.

To get E(DDLT > R) for use in (4-1), we must first employ (3-4) and determine the optimum reorder point for Q = 30.

$$P(DDLT > R) = \$495 \times .20 \times 30/(365 \times 40) = .203$$

. . . corresponding most closely to R = 3, for which E(DDLT > R) = .2764.

and now:

$$TACIM = [365/30 \times .2764 \times 40] + [(30/2 + 3\text{-}2) \times 495 \times .20]$$
$$+ [365/30 \times 20] + [365 \times 495] = \$182,636.85$$

---

[2]Except, of course, when demand is great enough to warrant buying at the base price. This will be dealt with in Chapter 6.

Our wholesaler now raises the question: "Would it pay to order Q = 56 units, and get into the *next* price bracket where CPU = $493?"

Once again, with (3-4) we determine the best reorder point for Q = 56 and the E(DDLT > R) associated with it:

$$P(DDLT > R) = \$493 \text{ x } .20 \text{ x } 56/(365 \text{ x } 40) = .202$$

. . . corresponding to R = 3, for which E(DDLT > R) = .2764, as before.

And now:

$$TACIM = [365/56 \text{ x } .2764 \text{ x } 40] + [(56/2 + 3\text{-}2) \text{ x } 493 \text{ x } .20]$$

$$+ [365/30 \text{ x } 20] + [365 \text{ x } 495] = \$182,636.85$$

Moving into the next price bracket would not pay.

In the analysis above our wholesaler assumed that his best policy

might be in the range Q = 2 through Q = 29, and therefore employed the per unit cost price for Item B corresponding to this order quantity range.

Let us assume that *prior* to doing any calculating he had a hunch that his optimum policy involved an order quantity in the range Q = 56 through 83. In using model (3-3) to get his first approximation of the optimum order quantity, he will employ as a per unit cost $495.

$$Q = \sqrt{\frac{2 \text{ x } 365 \text{ x } 20}{.20 \text{ x } 495}} = 12 \text{ units}$$

But Item B cannot be purchased in lots of this magnitude at CPU = $495.

Obviously, in searching for the best policy by use of models (3-3), (3-4), and (4-1), the *first* step is to search for a *"feasible"* policy. This will always be a policy which:

1. *satisfies (3-3) and (3-4); and*
2. *was calculated from (3-3) and (3-4) on the basis of a value for CPU which is specified in the delivered cost schedule for the resulting order quantity.*

a model for the case where backordering is not possible

Models (3-3), (3-4), and (4-1) are based on the assumption that backordering is permitted; that is, that when a stockout occurs the unfilled order enters a backorder queue (file) and is filled immediately out of the next shipment.

We interpret the case in which backordering is not permitted to mean that if units are demanded but not in stock, the order is filled by other means (pickup from a competing source of supply, perhaps) or it is lost entirely.

Models (3-3) and (4-1) are suitable for use where backordering is and where it is not permitted. Model (3-4) can, in some systems, be used for either of these two conditions, but for the case where backordering is not permitted the optimum reorder point can be approached with greater accuracy with the following altered form of (3-4):

$$P(DDLT > R) = \frac{CPU \times COP \times Q}{DPY \times SC + CPU \times COP \times Q}$$

If backordering is not permitted, and if a stockout occurs, the saving per reorder cycle attributable to increaseing the reorder point by *1 unit* consists of 2 elements:

1. *Reduced stockout cost, SC*
2. *Reduced holding cost*

We prevent a stockout by filling demand. We reduce our holding cost when we deliver a unit. If backordering is not permitted, element 2 therefore contributes to the total savings associated with increasing the reorder point by 1 unit.

Henceforth in the use of models (3-3), (3-4), and (4-1) we will assume that backordering is not permitted and we will use this form of model (3-4).

We addressed ourselves in the final section of this chapter to the development of a "practical method" for determining optimum policy in the inventory system under uncertainty with quantity extras. While "the practical method" we've developed is simpler than our former method of simply calculating costs associated with all reasonable policies, it is still rather involved. We will want to explore further short cuts. But first let us turn to the question: "Where does one acquire his demand during lead time probability distribution?"

The determination of the optimum reorder point depends chiefly on the demand during lead time distribution. In real systems we get our demand during lead time distribution from forecasts. In the next chapter we examine the forecasting process.

Table 4-1

With Expected Demand Per Year = 365 Units, At Delivered Cost of $495 Per Unit

Annual Materials Cost = $180,675

WITH REORDER POINT SET AT 2 UNITS

	AVERAGE INVENTORY	ANNUAL SHORTAGE	AHC	AOC	ASC	TAC	TAC INCLUDING MATERIALS COST
WHEN Q = 30 UNITS	15.0	7.6	1485.00	243.33	303.39	2031.72	182706.72
WHEN Q = 31 UNITS	15.5	7.3	1534.50	235.48	293.60	2063.59	182738.59
WHEN Q = 32 UNITS	16.0	7.1	1584.00	228.13	284.43	2096.55	182771.55
WHEN Q = 33 UNITS	16.5	6.9	1633.50	221.21	275.81	2130.52	182805.52
WHEN Q = 34 UNITS	17.0	6.7	1683.00	214.71	267.70	2165.40	182840.40
WHEN Q = 35 UNITS	17.5	6.5	1732.50	208.57	260.05	2201.12	182876.12
WHEN Q = 36 UNITS	18.0	6.3	1782.00	202.78	252.82	2237.60	182912.60
WHEN Q = 37 UNITS	18.5	6.1	1831.50	197.30	245.99	2274.79	182949.79
WHEN Q = 38 UNITS	19.0	6.0	1881.00	192.11	239.52	2312.62	182987.62
WHEN Q = 39 UNITS	19.5	5.8	1930.50	187.18	233.38	2351.05	183026.05
WHEN Q = 40 UNITS	20.0	5.7	1980.00	182.50	227.54	2390.04	183065.04
WHEN Q = 41 UNITS	20.5	5.5	2029.50	178.05	221.99	2429.54	183104.54
WHEN Q = 42 UNITS	21.0	5.4	2079.00	173.81	216.71	2469.52	183144.52
WHEN Q = 43 UNITS	21.5	5.3	2128.50	169.77	211.67	2509.93	183184.93
WHEN Q = 44 UNITS	22.0	5.2	2178.00	165.91	206.86	2550.76	183225.76
WHEN Q = 45 UNITS	22.5	5.1	2227.50	162.22	202.26	2591.98	183266.98
WHEN Q = 46 UNITS	23.0	4.9	2277.00	158.70	197.86	2633.56	183308.56
WHEN Q = 47 UNITS	23.5	4.8	2326.50	155.32	193.65	2675.47	183350.47
WHEN Q = 48 UNITS	24.0	4.7	2376.00	152.08	189.62	2717.70	183392.70
WHEN Q = 49 UNITS	24.5	4.6	2425.50	148.98	185.75	2760.23	183435.23
WHEN Q = 50 UNITS	25.0	4.6	2475.00	146.00	182.03	2803.03	183478.03
WHEN Q = 51 UNITS	25.5	4.5	2524.50	143.14	178.46	2846.10	183521.10
WHEN Q = 52 UNITS	26.0	4.4	2574.00	140.38	175.03	2889.42	183564.42
WHEN Q = 53 UNITS	26.5	4.3	2623.50	137.74	171.73	2932.96	183607.96
WHEN Q = 54 UNITS	27.0	4.2	2673.00	135.19	168.55	2976.73	183651.73
WHEN Q = 55 UNITS	27.5	4.1	2722.50	132.73	165.48	3020.71	183695.71

(Continued)

Table 4-1 (Continued)

WITH REORDER POINT SET AT 3 UNITS

	AVERAGE INVENTORY	ANNUAL SHORTAGE	AHC	AOC	ASC	TAC	TAC INCLUDING MATERIALS COST
WHEN Q = 30 UNITS	16.0	3.4	1584.00	243.33	134.51	1961.85	182636.85
WHEN Q = 31 UNITS	16.5	3.3	1633.50	235.48	130.18	1999.16	182674.16
WHEN Q = 32 UNITS	17.0	3.2	1683.00	228.13	126.11	2037.23	182712.23
WHEN Q = 33 UNITS	17.5	3.1	1732.50	221.21	122.29	2076.00	182751.00
WHEN Q = 34 UNITS	18.0	3.0	1782.00	214.71	118.69	2115.40	182790.40
WHEN Q = 35 UNITS	18.5	2.9	1831.50	208.57	115.30	2155.37	182830.37
WHEN Q = 36 UNITS	19.0	2.8	1881.00	202.78	112.10	2195.87	182870.87
WHEN Q = 37 UNITS	19.5	2.7	1930.50	197.30	109.07	2236.86	182911.86
WHEN Q = 38 UNITS	20.0	2.7	1980.00	192.11	106.20	2278.30	182953.30
WHEN Q = 39 UNITS	20.5	2.6	2029.50	187.18	103.47	2320.15	182995.15
WHEN Q = 40 UNITS	21.0	2.5	2079.00	182.50	100.89	2362.39	183037.39
WHEN Q = 41 UNITS	21.5	2.5	2128.50	178.05	98.43	2404.97	183079.97
WHEN Q = 42 UNITS	22.0	2.4	2178.00	173.81	96.08	2447.89	183122.89
WHEN Q = 43 UNITS	22.5	2.3	2227.50	169.77	93.85	2491.11	183166.11
WHEN Q = 44 UNITS	23.0	2.3	2277.00	165.91	91.71	2534.62	183209.62
WHEN Q = 45 UNITS	23.5	2.2	2326.50	162.22	89.68	2578.40	183253.40
WHEN Q = 46 UNITS	24.0	2.2	2376.00	158.70	87.73	2622.42	183297.42
WHEN Q = 47 UNITS	24.5	2.1	2425.50	155.32	85.86	2666.68	183341.68
WHEN Q = 48 UNITS	25.0	2.1	2475.00	152.08	84.07	2711.15	183386.16
WHEN Q = 49 UNITS	25.5	2.1	2524.50	148.98	82.36	2755.84	183430.84
WHEN Q = 50 UNITS	26.0	2.0	2574.00	146.00	80.71	2800.71	183475.71
WHEN Q = 51 UNITS	26.5	2.0	2623.50	143.14	79.13	2845.76	183520.76
WHEN Q = 52 UNITS	27.0	1.9	2673.00	140.38	77.60	2890.99	183565.99
WHEN Q = 53 UNITS	27.5	1.9	2722.50	137.74	76.14	2936.38	183611.38
WHEN Q = 54 UNITS	28.0	1.9	2772.00	135.19	74.73	2981.92	183656.92
WHEN Q = 55 UNITS	28.5	1.8	2821.50	132.73	73.37	3027.60	183702.60

(Continued)

Table 4-1 (Continued)

WITH REORDER POINT SET AT 4 UNITS

	AVERAGE INVENTORY	ANNUAL SHORTAGE	AHC	AOC	ASC	TAC	TAC INCLUDING MATERIALS COST
WHEN Q = 30 UNITS	17.0	1.3	1683.00	243.33	53.10	1979.43	182654.43
WHEN Q = 31 UNITS	17.5	1.3	1732.50	235.48	51.38	2019.37	182694.37
WHEN Q = 32 UNITS	18.0	1.2	1782.00	228.13	49.78	2059.90	182734.90
WHEN Q = 33 UNITS	18.5	1.2	1831.50	221.21	48.27	2100.98	182775.98
WHEN Q = 34 UNITS	19.0	1.2	1881.00	214.71	46.85	2142.55	182817.55
WHEN Q = 35 UNITS	19.5	1.1	1930.50	208.57	45.51	2184.58	182859.58
WHEN Q = 36 UNITS	20.0	1.1	1980.00	202.78	44.25	2227.02	182902.02
WHEN Q = 37 UNITS	20.5	1.1	2029.50	197.30	43.05	2269.85	182944.85
WHEN Q = 38 UNITS	21.0	1.0	2079.00	192.11	41.92	2313.02	182988.02
WHEN Q = 39 UNITS	21.5	1.0	2128.50	187.18	40.84	2356.52	183031.52
WHEN Q = 40 UNITS	22.0	1.0	2178.00	182.50	39.82	2400.32	183075.32
WHEN Q = 41 UNITS	22.5	1.0	2227.50	178.05	38.85	2444.40	183119.40
WHEN Q = 42 UNITS	23.0	.9	2277.00	173.81	37.93	2488.73	183163.73
WHEN Q = 43 UNITS	23.5	.9	2326.50	169.77	37.04	2533.31	183208.31
WHEN Q = 44 UNITS	24.0	.9	2376.00	165.91	36.20	2578.11	183253.11
WHEN Q = 45 UNITS	24.5	.9	2425.50	162.22	35.40	2623.12	183298.12
WHEN Q = 46 UNITS	25.0	.9	2475.00	158.70	34.63	2668.32	183343.32
WHEN Q = 47 UNITS	25.5	.8	2524.50	155.32	33.89	2713.71	183388.71
WHEN Q = 48 UNITS	26.0	.8	2574.00	152.08	33.18	2759.27	183434.27
WHEN Q = 49 UNITS	26.5	.8	2623.50	148.98	32.51	2804.99	183479.99
WHEN Q = 50 UNITS	27.0	.8	2673.00	146.00	31.86	2850.86	183525.86
WHEN Q = 51 UNITS	27.5	.8	2722.50	143.14	31.23	2896.87	183571.87
WHEN Q = 52 UNITS	28.0	.8	2772.00	140.38	30.63	2943.02	183618.02
WHEN Q = 53 UNITS	28.5	.8	2821.50	137.74	30.05	2989.29	183664.29
WHEN Q = 54 UNITS	29.0	.7	2871.00	135.19	29.50	3035.68	183710.68
WHEN Q = 55 UNITS	29.5	.7	2920.50	132.73	28.96	3082.19	183757.19

(Continued)

Table 4-1 (Continued)

WITH REORDER POINT SET AT 5 UNITS

	AVERAGE INVENTORY	ANNUAL SHORTAGE	AHC	AOC	ASC	TAC	TAC INCLUDING MATERIALS COST
WHEN Q = 30 UNITS	18.0	.4	1782.00	243.33	17.18	2042.51	182717.51
WHEN Q = 31 UNITS	18.5	.4	1831.50	235.48	16.63	2083.61	182758.61
WHEN Q = 32 UNITS	19.0	.4	1881.00	228.13	16.11	2125.23	182800.23
WHEN Q = 33 UNITS	19.5	.4	1930.50	221.21	15.62	2167.33	182842.33
WHEN Q = 34 UNITS	20.0	.4	1980.00	214.71	15.16	2209.86	182884.86
WHEN Q = 35 UNITS	20.5	.4	2029.50	208.57	14.73	2252.80	182927.80
WHEN Q = 36 UNITS	21.0	.4	2079.00	202.78	14.32	2296.09	182971.09
WHEN Q = 37 UNITS	21.5	.3	2128.50	197.30	13.93	2339.73	183014.73
WHEN Q = 38 UNITS	22.0	.3	2178.00	192.11	13.56	2383.67	183058.67
WHEN Q = 39 UNITS	22.5	.3	2227.50	187.18	13.21	2427.89	183102.89
WHEN Q = 40 UNITS	23.0	.3	2277.00	182.50	12.88	2472.38	183147.38
WHEN Q = 41 UNITS	23.5	.3	2326.50	178.05	12.57	2517.12	183192.12
WHEN Q = 42 UNITS	24.0	.3	2376.00	173.81	12.27	2562.08	183237.08
WHEN Q = 43 UNITS	24.5	.3	2425.50	169.77	11.99	2607.25	183282.25
WHEN Q = 44 UNITS	25.0	.3	2475.00	165.91	11.71	2652.62	183327.62
WHEN Q = 45 UNITS	25.5	.3	2524.50	162.22	11.45	2698.18	183373.18
WHEN Q = 46 UNITS	26.0	.3	2574.00	158.70	11.20	2743.90	183418.90
WHEN Q = 47 UNITS	26.5	.3	2623.50	155.32	10.97	2789.78	183464.78
WHEN Q = 48 UNITS	27.0	.3	2673.00	152.08	10.74	2835.82	183510.82
WHEN Q = 49 UNITS	27.5	.3	2722.50	148.98	10.52	2882.00	183557.00
WHEN Q = 50 UNITS	28.0	.3	2772.00	146.00	10.31	2928.31	183603.31
WHEN Q = 51 UNITS	28.5	.3	2821.50	143.14	10.11	2974.74	183649.74
WHEN Q = 52 UNITS	29.0	.2	2871.00	140.38	9.91	3021.30	183696.30
WHEN Q = 53 UNITS	29.5	.2	2920.50	137.74	9.72	3067.96	183742.96
WHEN Q = 54 UNITS	30.0	.2	2970.00	135.19	9.54	3114.73	183789.73
WHEN Q = 55 UNITS	30.5	.2	3019.50	132.73	9.37	3161.60	183836.60

(Continued)

Table 4-1 (Continued)

WITH REORDER POINT SET AT 6 UNITS

	AVERAGE INVENTORY	ANNUAL SHORTAGE	AHC	AOC	ASC	TAC	TAC INCLUDING MATERIALS COST
WHEN Q = 30 UNITS	19.0	.1	1881.00	243.33	4.48	2128.81	182803.81
WHEN Q = 31 UNITS	19.5	.1	1930.50	235.48	4.33	2170.32	182845.32
WHEN Q = 32 UNITS	20.0	.1	1980.00	228.13	4.20	2212.32	182887.32
WHEN Q = 33 UNITS	20.5	.1	2029.50	221.21	4.07	2254.78	182929.78
WHEN Q = 34 UNITS	21.0	.1	2079.00	214.71	3.95	2297.66	182972.66
WHEN Q = 35 UNITS	21.5	.1	2128.50	208.57	3.84	2340.91	183015.91
WHEN Q = 36 UNITS	22.0	.1	2178.00	202.78	3.73	2384.51	183059.51
WHEN Q = 37 UNITS	22.5	.1	2227.50	197.30	3.63	2428.43	183103.43
WHEN Q = 38 UNITS	23.0	.1	2277.00	192.11	3.53	2472.64	183147.64
WHEN Q = 39 UNITS	23.5	.1	2326.50	187.18	3.44	2517.12	183192.12
WHEN Q = 40 UNITS	24.0	.1	2376.00	182.50	3.36	2561.86	183236.86
WHEN Q = 41 UNITS	24.5	.1	2425.50	178.05	3.28	2606.82	183281.82
WHEN Q = 42 UNITS	25.0	.1	2475.00	173.81	3.20	2652.01	183327.01
WHEN Q = 43 UNITS	25.5	.1	2524.50	169.77	3.12	2697.39	183372.39
WHEN Q = 44 UNITS	26.0	.1	2574.00	165.91	3.05	2742.96	183417.96
WHEN Q = 45 UNITS	26.5	.1	2623.50	162.22	2.98	2788.71	183463.71
WHEN Q = 46 UNITS	27.0	.1	2673.00	158.70	2.92	2834.62	183509.62
WHEN Q = 47 UNITS	27.5	.1	2722.50	155.32	2.86	2880.68	183555.68
WHEN Q = 48 UNITS	28.0	.1	2772.00	152.08	2.80	2926.88	183601.88
WHEN Q = 49 UNITS	28.5	.1	2821.50	148.98	2.74	2973.22	183648.22
WHEN Q = 50 UNITS	29.0	.1	2871.00	146.00	2.69	3019.69	183694.69
WHEN Q = 51 UNITS	29.5	.1	2920.50	143.14	2.63	3066.27	183741.27
WHEN Q = 52 UNITS	30.0	.1	2970.00	140.38	2.58	3112.97	183787.97
WHEN Q = 53 UNITS	30.5	.1	3019.50	137.74	2.53	3159.77	183834.77
WHEN Q = 54 UNITS	31.0	.1	3069.00	135.19	2.49	3206.67	183881.67
WHEN Q = 55 UNITS	31.5	.1	3118.50	132.73	2.44	3253.67	183928.67

(Continued)

Table 4-1 (Continued)

WITH REORDER POINT SET AT 7 UNITS

	AVERAGE INVENTORY	ANNUAL SHORTAGE	AHC	AOC	ASC	TAC	TAC INCLUDING MATERIALS COST
WHEN Q = 30 UNITS	20.0	.0	1980.00	243.33	1.02	2224.36	182899.36
WHEN Q = 31 UNITS	20.5	.0	2029.50	235.48	.99	2265.97	182940.97
WHEN Q = 32 UNITS	21.0	.0	2079.00	228.13	.96	2308.08	182983.08
WHEN Q = 33 UNITS	21.5	.0	2128.50	221.21	.93	2350.64	183025.64
WHEN Q = 34 UNITS	22.0	.0	2178.00	214.71	.90	2393.61	183068.61
WHEN Q = 35 UNITS	22.5	.0	2227.50	208.57	.88	2436.95	183111.95
WHEN Q = 36 UNITS	23.0	.0	2277.00	202.78	.85	2480.63	183155.63
WHEN Q = 37 UNITS	23.5	.0	2326.50	197.30	.83	2524.63	183199.63
WHEN Q = 38 UNITS	24.0	.0	2376.00	192.11	.81	2568.91	183243.91
WHEN Q = 39 UNITS	24.5	.0	2425.50	187.18	.79	2613.47	183288.47
WHEN Q = 40 UNITS	25.0	.0	2475.00	182.50	.77	2658.27	183333.27
WHEN Q = 41 UNITS	25.5	.0	2524.50	178.05	.75	2703.30	183378.30
WHEN Q = 42 UNITS	26.0	.0	2574.00	173.81	.73	2748.54	183423.54
WHEN Q = 43 UNITS	26.5	.0	2623.50	169.77	.71	2793.98	183468.98
WHEN Q = 44 UNITS	27.0	.0	2673.00	165.91	.70	2839.61	183514.61
WHEN Q = 45 UNITS	27.5	.0	2722.50	162.22	.68	2885.40	183560.40
WHEN Q = 46 UNITS	28.0	.0	2772.00	158.70	.67	2931.36	183606.36
WHEN Q = 47 UNITS	28.5	.0	2821.50	155.32	.65	2977.47	183652.47
WHEN Q = 48 UNITS	29.0	.0	2871.00	152.08	.64	3023.72	183698.72
WHEN Q = 49 UNITS	29.5	.0	2920.50	148.98	.63	3070.11	183745.11
WHEN Q = 50 UNITS	30.0	.0	2970.00	146.00	.61	3116.61	183791.61
WHEN Q = 51 UNITS	30.5	.0	3019.50	143.14	.60	3163.24	183838.24
WHEN Q = 52 UNITS	31.0	.0	3069.00	140.38	.59	3209.97	183884.97
WHEN Q = 53 UNITS	31.5	.0	3118.50	137.74	.58	3256.81	183931.81
WHEN Q = 54 UNITS	32.0	.0	3168.00	135.19	.57	3303.75	183978.75
WHEN Q = 55 UNITS	32.5	.0	3217.50	132.73	.56	3350.78	184025.78

(Continued)

Table 4-1 (Continued)

WITH REORDER POINT SET AT 8 UNITS

	AVERAGE INVENTORY	ANNUAL SHORTAGE	AHC	AOC	ASC	TAC	TAC INCLUDING MATERIALS COST
WHEN Q = 30 UNITS	21.0	.0	2079.00	243.33	.15	2322.48	182997.48
WHEN Q = 31 UNITS	21.5	.0	2128.50	235.48	.14	2364.13	183039.13
WHEN Q = 32 UNITS	22.0	.0	2178.00	228.13	.14	2406.26	183081.26
WHEN Q = 33 UNITS	22.5	.0	2227.50	221.21	.13	2448.84	183123.84
WHEN Q = 34 UNITS	23.0	.0	2277.00	214.71	.13	2491.83	183166.83
WHEN Q = 35 UNITS	23.5	.0	2326.50	208.57	.13	2535.20	183210.20
WHEN Q = 36 UNITS	24.0	.0	2376.00	202.78	.13	2578.90	183253.90
WHEN Q = 37 UNITS	24.5	.0	2425.50	197.30	.12	2622.92	183297.92
WHEN Q = 38 UNITS	25.0	.0	2475.00	192.11	.12	2667.22	183342.22
WHEN Q = 39 UNITS	25.5	.0	2524.50	187.18	.11	2711.79	183386.79
WHEN Q = 40 UNITS	26.0	.0	2574.00	182.50	.11	2756.61	183431.61
WHEN Q = 41 UNITS	26.5	.0	2623.50	178.05	.11	2801.66	183476.66
WHEN Q = 42 UNITS	27.0	.0	2673.00	173.81	.10	2846.91	183521.91
WHEN Q = 43 UNITS	27.5	.0	2722.50	169.77	.10	2892.37	183567.37
WHEN Q = 44 UNITS	28.0	.0	2772.00	165.91	.10	2938.01	183613.01
WHEN Q = 45 UNITS	28.5	.0	2821.50	162.22	.10	2983.82	183658.82
WHEN Q = 46 UNITS	29.0	.0	2871.00	158.70	.10	3029.79	183704.79
WHEN Q = 47 UNITS	29.5	.0	2920.50	155.32	.09	3075.91	183750.91
WHEN Q = 48 UNITS	30.0	.0	2970.00	152.08	.09	3122.17	183797.17
WHEN Q = 49 UNITS	30.5	.0	3019.50	148.98	.09	3168.57	183843.57
WHEN Q = 50 UNITS	31.0	.0	3069.00	146.00	.09	3215.09	183890.09
WHEN Q = 51 UNITS	31.5	.0	3118.50	143.14	.09	3261.72	183936.72
WHEN Q = 52 UNITS	32.0	.0	3168.00	140.38	.08	3308.47	183983.47
WHEN Q = 53 UNITS	32.5	.0	3217.50	137.74	.08	3355.32	184030.32
WHEN Q = 54 UNITS	33.0	.0	3267.00	135.19	.08	3402.27	184077.27
WHEN Q = 55 UNITS	33.5	.0	3316.50	132.73	.08	3449.31	184124.31

(Continued)

Table 4-2
With Expected Demand Per Year = 365 Units, At Delivered Cost of $493 Per Unit
Annual Materials Cost = $179,945

WITH REORDER POINT SET AT 2 UNITS

	AVERAGE INVENTORY	ANNUAL SHORTAGE	AHC	AOC	ASC	TAC	TAC INCLUDING MATERIALS COST
WHEN Q = 56 UNITS	28.0	4.1	2760.80	130.36	162.53	3053.69	182998.69
WHEN Q = 57 UNITS	28.5	4.0	2810.10	128.07	159.68	3097.85	183042.85
WHEN Q = 58 UNITS	29.0	3.9	2859.40	125.86	156.92	3142.19	183087.19
WHEN Q = 59 UNITS	29.5	3.9	2908.70	123.73	154.27	3186.69	183131.69
WHEN Q = 60 UNITS	30.0	3.8	2958.00	121.67	151.69	3231.36	183176.36
WHEN Q = 61 UNITS	30.5	3.7	3007.30	119.67	149.21	3276.18	183221.18
WHEN Q = 62 UNITS	31.0	3.7	3056.60	117.74	146.80	3321.14	183266.14
WHEN Q = 63 UNITS	31.5	3.6	3105.90	115.87	144.47	3366.24	183311.24
WHEN Q = 64 UNITS	32.0	3.6	3155.20	114.06	142.21	3411.48	183356.48
WHEN Q = 65 UNITS	32.5	3.5	3204.50	112.31	140.03	3456.83	183401.83
WHEN Q = 66 UNITS	33.0	3.4	3253.80	110.61	137.90	3502.31	183447.31
WHEN Q = 67 UNITS	33.5	3.4	3303.10	108.96	135.85	3547.90	183492.90
WHEN Q = 68 UNITS	34.0	3.3	3352.40	107.35	133.85	3593.60	183538.60
WHEN Q = 69 UNITS	34.5	3.3	3401.70	105.80	131.91	3639.40	183584.40
WHEN Q = 70 UNITS	35.0	3.3	3451.00	104.29	130.02	3685.31	183630.31
WHEN Q = 71 UNITS	35.5	3.2	3500.30	102.82	128.19	3731.31	183676.31
WHEN Q = 72 UNITS	36.0	3.2	3549.60	101.39	126.41	3777.40	183722.40
WHEN Q = 73 UNITS	36.5	3.1	3598.90	100.00	124.68	3823.58	183768.58
WHEN Q = 74 UNITS	37.0	3.1	3648.20	98.65	123.00	3869.84	183814.84
WHEN Q = 75 UNITS	37.5	3.0	3697.50	97.33	121.36	3916.19	183861.19
WHEN Q = 76 UNITS	38.0	3.0	3746.80	96.05	119.76	3962.61	183907.61
WHEN Q = 77 UNITS	38.5	3.0	3796.10	94.81	118.20	4009.11	183954.11
WHEN Q = 78 UNITS	39.0	2.9	3845.40	93.59	116.68	4055.68	184000.68
WHEN Q = 79 UNITS	39.5	2.9	3894.70	92.41	115.21	4102.32	184047.32
WHEN Q = 80 UNITS	40.0	2.8	3944.00	91.25	113.77	4149.02	184094.02
WHEN Q = 81 UNITS	40.5	2.8	3993.30	90.12	112.37	4195.79	184140.79
WHEN Q = 82 UNITS	41.0	2.8	4042.60	89.02	111.00	4242.62	184187.62
WHEN Q = 83 UNITS	41.5	2.7	4091.90	87.95	109.66	4289.51	184234.51

(Continued)

Table 4-2 (Continued)

WITH REORDER POINT SET AT 3 UNITS

	AVERAGE INVENTORY	ANNUAL SHORTAGE	AHC	AOC	ASC	TAC	TAC INCLUDING MATERIALS COST
WHEN Q = 56 UNITS	29.0	1.8	2859.40	130.36	72.06	3061.82	183006.82
WHEN Q = 57 UNITS	29.5	1.8	2908.70	128.07	70.80	3107.57	183052.57
WHEN Q = 58 UNITS	30.0	1.7	2958.00	125.86	69.58	3153.44	183098.44
WHEN Q = 59 UNITS	30.5	1.7	3007.30	123.73	68.40	3199.43	183144.43
WHEN Q = 60 UNITS	31.0	1.7	3056.60	121.67	67.26	3245.52	183190.52
WHEN Q = 61 UNITS	31.5	1.7	3105.90	119.67	66.15	3291.73	183236.73
WHEN Q = 62 UNITS	32.0	1.6	3155.20	117.74	65.09	3338.03	183283.03
WHEN Q = 63 UNITS	32.5	1.6	3204.50	115.87	64.05	3384.43	183329.43
WHEN Q = 64 UNITS	33.0	1.6	3253.80	114.06	63.05	3430.92	183375.92
WHEN Q = 65 UNITS	33.5	1.6	3303.10	112.31	62.08	3477.49	183422.49
WHEN Q = 66 UNITS	34.0	1.5	3352.40	110.61	61.14	3524.15	183469.15
WHEN Q = 67 UNITS	34.5	1.5	3401.70	108.96	60.23	3570.89	183515.89
WHEN Q = 68 UNITS	35.0	1.5	3451.00	107.35	59.34	3617.70	183562.70
WHEN Q = 69 UNITS	35.5	1.5	3500.30	105.80	58.48	3664.58	183609.58
WHEN Q = 70 UNITS	36.0	1.4	3549.60	104.29	57.65	3711.53	183656.53
WHEN Q = 71 UNITS	36.5	1.4	3598.90	102.82	56.84	3758.55	183703.55
WHEN Q = 72 UNITS	37.0	1.4	3648.20	101.39	56.05	3805.64	183750.64
WHEN Q = 73 UNITS	37.5	1.4	3697.50	100.00	55.28	3852.78	183797.78
WHEN Q = 74 UNITS	38.0	1.4	3746.80	98.65	54.53	3899.98	183844.98
WHEN Q = 75 UNITS	38.5	1.3	3796.10	97.33	53.81	3947.24	183892.24
WHEN Q = 76 UNITS	39.0	1.3	3845.40	96.05	53.10	3994.55	183939.55
WHEN Q = 77 UNITS	39.5	1.3	3894.70	94.81	52.41	4041.91	183986.91
WHEN Q = 78 UNITS	40.0	1.3	3944.00	93.59	51.74	4089.33	184034.33
WHEN Q = 79 UNITS	40.5	1.3	3993.30	92.41	51.08	4136.79	184081.79
WHEN Q = 80 UNITS	41.0	1.3	4042.60	91.25	50.44	4184.29	184129.29
WHEN Q = 81 UNITS	41.5	1.2	4091.90	90.12	49.82	4231.84	184176.84
WHEN Q = 82 UNITS	42.0	1.2	4141.20	89.02	49.21	4279.44	184224.44
WHEN Q = 83 UNITS	42.5	1.2	4190.50	87.95	48.62	4327.07	184272.07

(Continued)

Table 4-2 (Continued)

WITH REORDER POINT SET AT 4 UNITS

	AVERAGE INVENTORY	ANNUAL SHORTAGE	AHC	AOC	ASC	TAC	TAC INCLUDING MATERIALS COST
WHEN Q = 56 UNITS	30.0	.7	2958.00	130.36	28.44	3116.80	183061.80
WHEN Q = 57 UNITS	30.5	.7	3007.30	128.07	27.94	3163.32	183108.32
WHEN Q = 58 UNITS	31.0	.7	3056.60	125.86	27.46	3209.93	183154.93
WHEN Q = 59 UNITS	31.5	.7	3105.90	123.73	27.00	3256.63	183201.63
WHEN Q = 60 UNITS	32.0	.7	3155.20	121.67	26.55	3303.41	183248.41
WHEN Q = 61 UNITS	32.5	.7	3204.50	119.67	26.11	3350.28	183295.28
WHEN Q = 62 UNITS	33.0	.6	3253.80	117.74	25.69	3397.23	183342.23
WHEN Q = 63 UNITS	33.5	.6	3303.10	115.87	25.28	3444.26	183389.26
WHEN Q = 64 UNITS	34.0	.6	3352.40	114.06	24.89	3491.35	183436.35
WHEN Q = 65 UNITS	34.5	.6	3401.70	112.31	24.51	3538.51	183483.51
WHEN Q = 66 UNITS	35.0	.6	3451.00	110.61	24.13	3585.74	183530.74
WHEN Q = 67 UNITS	35.5	.6	3500.30	108.96	23.77	3633.03	183578.03
WHEN Q = 68 UNITS	36.0	.6	3549.60	107.35	23.42	3680.38	183625.38
WHEN Q = 69 UNITS	36.5	.6	3598.90	105.80	23.08	3727.78	183672.78
WHEN Q = 70 UNITS	37.0	.6	3648.20	104.29	22.76	3775.24	183720.24
WHEN Q = 71 UNITS	37.5	.6	3697.50	102.82	22.43	3822.75	183767.75
WHEN Q = 72 UNITS	38.0	.6	3746.80	101.39	22.12	3870.31	183815.31
WHEN Q = 73 UNITS	38.5	.5	3796.10	100.00	21.82	3917.92	183862.92
WHEN Q = 74 UNITS	39.0	.5	3845.40	98.65	21.53	3965.57	183910.57
WHEN Q = 75 UNITS	39.5	.5	3894.70	97.33	21.24	4013.27	183958.27
WHEN Q = 76 UNITS	40.0	.5	3944.00	96.05	20.96	4061.01	184006.01
WHEN Q = 77 UNITS	40.5	.5	3993.30	94.81	20.69	4108.79	184053.79
WHEN Q = 78 UNITS	41.0	.5	4042.60	93.59	20.42	4156.61	194101.61
WHEN Q = 79 UNITS	41.5	.5	4091.90	92.41	20.16	4204.47	184149.47
WHEN Q = 80 UNITS	42.0	.5	4141.20	91.25	19.91	4252.36	184197.36
WHEN Q = 81 UNITS	42.5	.5	4190.50	90.12	19.66	4300.29	184245.29
WHEN Q = 82 UNITS	43.0	.5	4239.80	89.02	19.43	4348.25	184293.25
WHEN Q = 83 UNITS	43.5	.5	4289.10	87.95	19.19	4396.24	184341.24

(Continued)

Table 4-2 (Continued)

WITH REORDER POINT SET AT 5 UNITS

	AVERAGE INVENTORY	ANNUAL SHORTAGE	AHC	AOC	ASC	TAC	TAC INCLUDING MATERIALS COST
WHEN Q = 56 UNITS	31.0	.2	3056.60	130.36	9.20	3196.16	183141.16
WHEN Q = 57 UNITS	31.5	.2	3105.90	128.07	9.04	3243.01	183188.01
WHEN Q = 58 UNITS	32.0	.2	3155.20	125.86	8.89	3289.95	183234.95
WHEN Q = 59 UNITS	32.5	.2	3204.50	123.73	8.74	3336.96	183281.96
WHEN Q = 60 UNITS	33.0	.2	3253.80	121.67	8.59	3384.06	183329.06
WHEN Q = 61 UNITS	33.5	.2	3303.10	119.67	8.45	3431.22	183376.22
WHEN Q = 62 UNITS	34.0	.2	3352.40	117.74	8.31	3478.45	183423.45
WHEN Q = 63 UNITS	34.5	.2	3401.70	115.87	8.18	3525.75	183470.75
WHEN Q = 64 UNITS	35.0	.2	3451.00	114.06	8.05	3573.12	183518.12
WHEN Q = 65 UNITS	35.5	.2	3500.30	112.31	7.93	3620.54	183565.54
WHEN Q = 66 UNITS	36.0	.2	3549.60	110.61	7.81	3668.01	183613.01
WHEN Q = 67 UNITS	36.5	.2	3598.90	108.96	7.69	3715.55	183660.55
WHEN Q = 68 UNITS	37.0	.2	3648.20	107.35	7.58	3763.13	183708.13
WHEN Q = 69 UNITS	37.5	.2	3697.50	105.80	7.47	3810.77	183755.77
WHEN Q = 70 UNITS	38.0	.2	3746.80	104.29	7.36	3858.45	183803.45
WHEN Q = 71 UNITS	38.5	.2	3796.10	102.82	7.26	3906.18	183851.18
WHEN Q = 72 UNITS	39.0	.2	3845.40	101.39	7.16	3953.95	183898.95
WHEN Q = 73 UNITS	39.5	.2	3894.70	100.00	7.06	4001.76	183946.76
WHEN Q = 74 UNITS	40.0	.2	3944.00	98.65	6.96	4049.61	183994.61
WHEN Q = 75 UNITS	40.5	.2	3993.30	97.33	6.87	4097.51	184042.51
WHEN Q = 76 UNITS	41.0	.2	4042.60	96.05	6.78	4145.43	184090.43
WHEN Q = 77 UNITS	41.5	.2	4091.90	94.81	6.69	4193.40	184138.40
WHEN Q = 78 UNITS	43.0	.2	4141.20	93.59	6.61	4241.40	184186.40
WHEN Q = 79 UNITS	42.5	.2	4190.50	92.41	6.52	4289.43	184234.43
WHEN Q = 80 UNITS	43.0	.2	4239.80	91.25	6.44	4337.49	184282.49
WHEN Q = 81 UNITS	43.5	.2	4289.10	90.12	6.36	4385.59	184330.59
WHEN Q = 82 UNITS	44.0	.2	4338.40	89.02	6.29	4433.71	184378.71
WHEN Q = 83 UNITS	44.5	.2	4387.70	87.95	6.21	4481.86	184426.86

(Continued)

Table 4-2 (Continued)

WITH REORDER POINT SET AT 6 UNITS

	AVERAGE INVENTORY	ANNUAL SHORTAGE	AHC	AOC	ASC	TAC	TAC INCLUDING MATERIALS COST
WHEN Q = 56 UNITS	32.0	.1	3155.20	130.36	2.40	3287.96	183232.96
WHEN Q = 57 UNITS	32.5	.1	3204.50	128.07	2.36	3334.93	183279.93
WHEN Q = 58 UNITS	33.0	.1	3253.80	125.86	2.32	3381.98	183326.98
WHEN Q = 59 UNITS	33.5	.1	3303.10	123.73	2.28	3429.11	183374.11
WHEN Q = 60 UNITS	34.0	.1	3352.40	121.67	2.24	3476.31	183421.31
WHEN Q = 61 UNITS	34.5	.1	3401.70	119.67	2.20	3523.57	183468.57
WHEN Q = 62 UNITS	35.0	.1	3451.00	117.74	2.17	3570.91	183515.91
WHEN Q = 63 UNITS	35.5	.1	3500.30	115.87	2.13	3618.31	183563.31
WHEN Q = 64 UNITS	36.0	.1	3549.60	114.06	2.10	3665.76	183610.76
WHEN Q = 65 UNITS	36.5	.1	3598.90	112.31	2.07	3713.27	183658.27
WHEN Q = 66 UNITS	37.0	.1	3648.20	110.61	2.04	3760.84	183705.84
WHEN Q = 67 UNITS	37.5	.1	3697.50	108.96	2.00	3808.46	183753.46
WHEN Q = 68 UNITS	38.0	.0	3746.80	107.35	1.98	3856.13	183801.13
WHEN Q = 69 UNITS	38.5	.0	3796.10	105.80	1.95	3903.84	183848.84
WHEN Q = 70 UNITS	39.0	.0	3845.40	104.29	1.92	3951.60	183896.60
WHEN Q = 71 UNITS	39.5	.0	3894.70	102.82	1.89	3999.41	183944.41
WHEN Q = 72 UNITS	40.0	.0	3944.00	101.39	1.87	4047.25	183992.25
WHEN Q = 73 UNITS	40.5	.0	3993.30	100.00	1.84	4095.14	184040.14
WHEN Q = 74 UNITS	41.0	.0	4042.60	98.65	1.82	4143.06	184088.06
WHEN Q = 75 UNITS	41.5	.0	4091.90	97.33	1.79	4191.02	184136.02
WHEN Q = 76 UNITS	42.0	.0	4141.20	96.05	1.77	4239.02	184184.02
WHEN Q = 77 UNITS	42.5	.0	4190.50	94.81	1.74	4287.05	184232.05
WHEN Q = 78 UNITS	43.0	.0	4239.80	93.59	1.72	4335.11	184280.11
WHEN Q = 79 UNITS	43.5	.0	4289.10	92.41	1.70	4383.21	184328.21
WHEN Q = 80 UNITS	44.0	.0	4338.40	91.25	1.68	4431.33	184376.33
WHEN Q = 81 UNITS	44.5	.0	4387.70	90.12	1.66	4479.48	184424.48
WHEN Q = 82 UNITS	45.0	.0	4437.00	89.02	1.64	4527.66	184472.66
WHEN Q = 83 UNITS	45.5	.0	4486.30	87.95	1.62	4575.87	184520.87

(Continued)

Table 4-2 (Continued)

WITH REORDER POINT SET AT 7 UNITS

	AVERAGE INVENTORY	ANNUAL SHORTAGE	AHC	AOC	ASC	TAC	TAC INCLUDING MATERIALS COST
WHEN Q = 56 UNITS	33.0	.0	3253.80	130.36	.55	3384.70	183329.70
WHEN Q = 57 UNITS	33.5	.0	3303.10	128.07	.54	3431.71	183376.71
WHEN Q = 58 UNITS	34.0	.0	3352.40	125.86	.53	3478.79	183423.79
WHEN Q = 59 UNITS	34.5	.0	3401.70	123.73	.52	3525.95	183470.95
WHEN Q = 60 UNITS	35.0	.0	3451.00	121.67	.51	3573.18	183518.18
WHEN Q = 61 UNITS	35.5	.0	3500.30	119.67	.50	3620.47	183565.47
WHEN Q = 62 UNITS	36.0	.0	3549.60	117.74	.49	3667.84	183612.84
WHEN Q = 63 UNITS	36.5	.0	3598.90	115.87	.49	3715.26	183660.26
WHEN Q = 64 UNITS	37.0	.0	3648.20	114.06	.48	3762.74	183707.74
WHEN Q = 65 UNITS	37.5	.0	3697.50	112.31	.47	3810.28	183755.28
WHEN Q = 66 UNITS	38.0	.0	3746.80	110.61	.46	3857.87	183802.87
WHEN Q = 67 UNITS	38.5	.0	3796.10	108.96	.46	3905.51	183850.51
WHEN Q = 68 UNITS	39.0	.0	3845.40	107.35	.45	3953.20	183898.20
WHEN Q = 69 UNITS	39.5	.0	3894.70	105.80	.44	4000.94	183945.94
WHEN Q = 70 UNITS	40.0	.0	3944.00	104.29	.44	4048.72	183993.72
WHEN Q = 71 UNITS	40.5	.0	3993.30	102.82	.43	4096.55	184041.55
WHEN Q = 72 UNITS	41.0	.0	4042.60	101.39	.43	4144.41	184089.41
WHEN Q = 73 UNITS	41.5	.0	4091.90	100.00	.42	4192.32	184137.32
WHEN Q = 74 UNITS	42.0	.0	4141.20	98.65	.41	4240.26	184185.26
WHEN Q = 75 UNITS	42.5	.0	4190.50	97.33	.41	4288.24	184233.24
WHEN Q = 76 UNITS	43.0	.0	4239.80	96.05	.40	4336.26	184281.26
WHEN Q = 77 UNITS	43.5	.0	4289.10	94.81	.40	4384.30	184329.30
WHEN Q = 78 UNITS	44.0	.0	4338.40	93.59	.39	4432.38	184377.38
WHEN Q = 79 UNITS	44.5	.0	4387.70	92.41	.39	4480.49	184425.49
WHEN Q = 80 UNITS	45.0	.0	4437.00	91.25	.38	4528.63	184473.63
WHEN Q = 81 UNITS	45.5	.0	4486.30	90.12	.38	4576.80	184521.80
WHEN Q = 82 UNITS	46.0	.0	4535.60	89.02	.37	4625.00	184570.00
WHEN Q = 83 UNITS	46.5	.0	4584.90	87.95	.37	4673.22	184618.22

(Continued)

MANAGEMENT

Table 4-2 (Continued)

WITH REORDER POINT SET AT 8 UNITS

	AVERAGE INVENTORY	ANNUAL SHORTAGE	AHC	AOC	ASC	TAC	TAC INCLUDING MATERIALS COST
WHEN Q = 56 UNITS	34.0	.0	3352.40	130.36	.08	3482.84	183427.84
WHEN Q = 57 UNITS	34.5	.0	3401.70	128.07	.08	3529.85	183474.85
WHEN Q = 58 UNITS	35.0	.0	3451.00	125.86	.08	3576.94	183521.94
WHEN Q = 59 UNITS	35.5	.0	3500.30	123.73	.07	3624.10	183569.10
WHEN Q = 60 UNITS	36.0	.0	3549.60	121.67	.07	3671.34	183616.34
WHEN Q = 61 UNITS	36.5	.0	3598.90	119.67	.07	3718.64	183663.64
WHEN Q = 62 UNITS	37.0	.0	3648.20	117.74	.07	3766.01	183711.01
WHEN Q = 63 UNITS	37.5	.0	3697.50	115.87	.07	3813.44	183758.44
WHEN Q = 64 UNITS	38.0	.0	3746.80	114.06	.07	3860.93	183805.93
WHEN Q = 65 UNITS	38.5	.0	3796.10	112.31	.07	3908.48	183853.48
WHEN Q = 66 UNITS	39.0	.0	3845.40	110.61	.07	3956.07	183901.07
WHEN Q = 67 UNITS	39.5	.0	3894.70	108.96	.07	4003.72	183948.72
WHEN Q = 68 UNITS	40.0	.0	3944.00	107.35	.06	4051.42	183996.42
WHEN Q = 69 UNITS	40.5	.0	3993.30	105.80	.06	4099.16	184044.16
WHEN Q = 70 UNITS	41.0	.0	4042.60	104.29	.06	4146.95	184091.95
WHEN Q = 71 UNITS	41.5	.0	4091.90	102.82	.06	4194.78	184139.78
WHEN Q = 72 UNITS	42.0	.0	4141.20	101.39	.06	4242.65	184187.65
WHEN Q = 73 UNITS	42.5	.0	4190.50	100.00	.06	4290.56	184235.56
WHEN Q = 74 UNITS	43.0	.0	4239.80	98.65	.06	4338.51	184283.51
WHEN Q = 75 UNITS	43.5	.0	4289.10	97.33	.06	4386.49	184331.49
WHEN Q = 76 UNITS	44.0	.0	4338.40	96.05	.06	4434.51	184379.51
WHEN Q = 77 UNITS	44.5	.0	4387.70	94.81	.06	4482.56	184427.56
WHEN Q = 78 UNITS	45.0	.0	4437.00	93.59	.06	4530.65	184475.65
WHEN Q = 79 UNITS	45.5	.0	4486.30	92.41	.06	4578.76	184523.76
WHEN Q = 80 UNITS	46.0	.0	4535.60	91.25	.05	4626.90	184571.90
WHEN Q = 81 UNITS	46.5	.0	4584.90	90.12	.05	4675.08	184620.08
WHEN Q = 82 UNITS	47.0	.0	4634.20	89.02	.05	4723.28	184668.28
WHEN Q = 83 UNITS	47.5	.0	4683.50	87.95	.05	4771.50	184716.50

Table 4-3

With Expected Demand Per Year = 365 Units, At Delivered Cost of $492 Per Unit
Annual Materials Cost = $179,580

WITH REORDER POINT SET AT 2 UNITS

	AVERAGE INVENTORY	ANNUAL SHORTAGE	AHC	AOC	ASC	TAC	TAC INCLUDING MATERIALS COST
WHEN Q = 84 UNITS	42.0	2.7	4132.80	86.90	108.35	4328.06	183908.06
WHEN Q = 85 UNITS	42.5	2.7	4182.00	85.88	107.08	4374.96	183954.96
WHEN Q = 86 UNITS	43.0	2.6	4231.20	84.88	105.83	4421.92	184001.92
WHEN Q = 87 UNITS	43.5	2.6	4280.40	83.91	104.62	4468.92	184048.92
WHEN Q = 88 UNITS	44.0	2.6	4329.60	82.95	103.43	4515.98	184095.98
WHEN Q = 89 UNITS	44.5	2.6	4378.80	82.02	102.27	4563.09	184143.09
WHEN Q = 90 UNITS	45.0	2.5	4428.00	81.11	101.13	4610.24	184190.24
WHEN Q = 91 UNITS	45.5	2.5	4477.20	80.22	100.02	4657.44	184237.44
WHEN Q = 92 UNITS	46.0	2.5	4526.40	79.35	98.93	4704.68	184284.68
WHEN Q = 93 UNITS	46.5	2.4	4575.60	78.49	97.87	4751.96	184331.96
WHEN Q = 94 UNITS	47.0	2.4	4624.80	77.66	96.83	4799.29	184379.29
WHEN Q = 95 UNITS	47.5	2.4	4674.00	76.84	95.81	4846.65	184426.65
WHEN Q = 96 UNITS	48.0	2.4	4723.20	76.04	94.81	4894.05	184474.05
WHEN Q = 97 UNITS	48.5	2.3	4772.40	75.26	93.83	4941.49	184521.49
WHEN Q = 98 UNITS	49.0	2.3	4821.60	74.49	92.87	4988.96	184568.96
WHEN Q = 99 UNITS	49.5	2.3	4870.80	73.74	91.94	5036.47	184616.47
WHEN Q = 100 UNITS	50.0	2.3	4920.00	73.00	91.02	5084.02	184664.02
WHEN Q = 101 UNITS	50.5	2.3	4969.20	72.28	90.12	5131.59	184711.59
WHEN Q = 102 UNITS	51.0	2.2	5018.40	71.57	89.23	5179.20	184759.20
WHEN Q = 103 UNITS	51.5	2.2	5067.60	70.87	88.37	5226.84	184806.84
WHEN Q = 104 UNITS	52.0	2.2	5116.80	70.19	87.52	5274.51	184854.51
WHEN Q = 105 UNITS	52.5	2.2	5166.00	69.52	86.68	5322.21	184902.21
WHEN Q = 106 UNITS	53.0	2.1	5215.20	68.87	85.86	5369.93	184949.93
WHEN Q = 107 UNITS	53.5	2.1	5264.40	68.22	85.06	5417.69	184997.69
WHEN Q = 108 UNITS	54.0	2.1	5313.60	67.59	84.27	5465.47	185045.47
WHEN Q = 109 UNITS	54.5	2.1	5362.80	66.97	83.50	5513.27	185093.27
WHEN Q = 110 UNITS	55.0	2.1	5412.00	66.36	82.74	5561.11	185141.11

(Continued)

Table 4-3 (Continued)

WITH REORDER POINT SET AT 3 UNITS

	AVERAGE INVENTORY	ANNUAL SHORTAGE	AHC	AOC	ASC	TAC	TAC INCLUDING MATERIALS COST
WHEN Q = 84 UNITS	43.0	1.2	4231.20	86.90	48.04	4366.15	183946.15
WHEN Q = 85 UNITS	43.5	1.2	4280.40	85.88	47.48	4413.76	183993.76
WHEN Q = 86 UNITS	44.0	1.2	4329.60	84.88	46.92	4461.41	184041.41
WHEN Q = 87 UNITS	44.5	1.2	4378.80	83.91	46.38	4509.09	184089.09
WHEN Q = 88 UNITS	45.0	1.1	4428.00	82.95	45.86	4556.81	184136.81
WHEN Q = 89 UNITS	45.5	1.1	4477.20	82.02	45.34	4604.56	184184.56
WHEN Q = 90 UNITS	46.0	1.1	4526.40	81.11	44.84	4652.35	184232.35
WHEN Q = 91 UNITS	46.5	1.1	4575.60	80.22	44.35	4700.17	184280.17
WHEN Q = 92 UNITS	47.0	1.1	4624.80	79.35	43.86	4748.01	184328.01
WHEN Q = 93 UNITS	47.5	1.1	4674.00	78.49	43.39	4795.89	184375.89
WHEN Q = 94 UNITS	48.0	1.1	4723.20	77.66	42.93	4843.79	184423.79
WHEN Q = 95 UNITS	48.5	1.1	4772.40	76.84	42.48	4891.72	184471.72
WHEN Q = 96 UNITS	49.0	1.1	4821.60	76.04	42.04	4939.68	184519.68
WHEN Q = 97 UNITS	49.5	1.0	4870.80	75.26	41.60	4987.66	184567.66
WHEN Q = 98 UNITS	50.0	1.0	4920.00	74.49	41.18	5035.67	184615.67
WHEN Q = 99 UNITS	50.5	1.0	4969.20	73.74	40.76	5083.70	184663.70
WHEN Q = 100 UNITS	51.0	1.0	5018.40	72.28	39.95	5179.83	184759.83
WHEN Q = 101 UNITS	51.5	1.0	5067.60	71.57	39.56	5227.93	184807.93
WHEN Q = 102 UNITS	52.0	1.0	5116.80	70.87	39.18	5276.05	184856.05
WHEN Q = 103 UNITS	52.5	1.0	5166.00	70.19	38.80	5324.19	184904.19
WHEN Q = 104 UNITS	53.0	1.0	5215.20	73.00	40.35	5131.75	184711.75
WHEN Q = 105 UNITS	53.5	1.0	5264.40	69.52	38.43	5372.36	184952.36
WHEN Q = 106 UNITS	54.0	1.0	5313.60	68.87	38.07	5420.54	185000.54
WHEN Q = 107 UNITS	54.5	.9	5362.80	68.22	37.71	5468.74	185048.74
WHEN Q = 108 UNITS	55.0	.9	5412.00	67.59	37.37	5516.96	185096.96
WHEN Q = 109 UNITS	55.5	.9	5461.20	66.97	37.02	5565.19	185145.19
WHEN Q = 110 UNITS	56.0	.9	5510.40	66.36	36.69	5613.45	185193.45

(Continued)

Table 4-3 (Continued)

WITH REORDER POINT SET AT 4 UNITS

	AVERAGE INVENTORY	ANNUAL SHORTAGE	AHC	AOC	ASC	TAC	TAC INCLUDING MATERIALS COST
WHEN Q = 84 UNITS	44.0	.5	4329.60	86.90	18.96	4435.47	184015.47
WHEN Q = 85 UNITS	44.5	.5	4378.80	85.88	18.74	4483.42	184063.42
WHEN Q = 86 UNITS	45.0	.5	4428.00	84.88	18.52	4531.41	184111.41
WHEN Q = 87 UNITS	45.5	.5	4477.20	83.91	18.31	4579.42	184159.42
WHEN Q = 88 UNITS	46.0	.5	4526.40	82.95	18.10	4627.46	184207.46
WHEN Q = 89 UNITS	46.5	.4	4575.60	82.02	17.90	4675.52	184255.52
WHEN Q = 90 UNITS	47.0	.4	4624.80	81.11	17.70	4723.61	184303.61
WHEN Q = 91 UNITS	47.5	.4	4674.00	80.22	17.50	4771.72	184351.72
WHEN Q = 92 UNITS	48.0	.4	4723.20	79.35	17.31	4819.86	184399.86
WHEN Q = 93 UNITS	48.5	.4	4772.40	78.49	17.13	4868.02	184448.02
WHEN Q = 94 UNITS	49.0	.4	4821.60	77.66	16.95	4916.20	184496.20
WHEN Q = 95 UNITS	49.5	.4	4870.80	76.84	16.77	4964.41	184544.41
WHEN Q = 96 UNITS	50.0	.4	4920.00	76.04	16.59	5012.63	184592.63
WHEN Q = 97 UNITS	50.5	.4	4969.20	75.26	16.42	5060.88	184640.88
WHEN Q = 98 UNITS	51.0	.4	5018.40	74.49	16.25	5109.14	184689.41
WHEN Q = 99 UNITS	51.5	.4	5067.60	73.74	16.09	5157.43	184737.43
WHEN Q = 100 UNITS	52.0	.4	5116.80	73.00	15.93	5205.73	184785.73
WHEN Q = 101 UNITS	52.5	.4	5166.00	72.28	15.77	5254.05	184834.05
WHEN Q = 102 UNITS	53.0	.4	5215.20	71.57	15.62	5302.38	184882.38
WHEN Q = 103 UNITS	53.5	.4	5264.40	70.87	15.46	5350.74	184930.74
WHEN Q = 104 UNITS	54.0	.4	5313.60	70.19	15.32	5399.11	184979.11
WHEN Q = 105 UNITS	54.5	.4	5362.80	69.52	15.17	5447.49	185027.49
WHEN Q = 106 UNITS	55.0	.4	5412.00	68.87	15.03	5495.89	185075.89
WHEN Q = 107 UNITS	55.5	.4	5461.20	68.22	14.89	5544.31	185124.31
WHEN Q = 108 UNITS	56.0	.4	5510.40	67.59	14.75	5592.74	185172.74
WHEN Q = 109 UNITS	56.5	.4	5559.60	66.97	14.61	5641.19	185221.19
WHEN Q = 110 UNITS	57.0	.4	5608.80	66.36	14.48	5689.64	185269.64

(Continued)

Table 4-3 (Continued)

WITH REORDER POINT SET AT 5 UNITS

	AVERAGE INVENTORY	ANNUAL SHORTAGE	AHC	AOC	ASC	TAC	TAC INCLUDING MATERIALS COST
WHEN Q = 84 UNITS	45.0	.2	4428.00	86.90	6.14	4521.04	184101.04
WHEN Q = 85 UNITS	45.5	.2	4477.20	85.88	6.06	4569.15	184149.15
WHEN Q = 86 UNITS	46.0	.1	4526.40	84.88	5.99	4617.28	184197.28
WHEN Q = 87 UNITS	46.5	.1	4575.60	83.91	5.92	4665.43	184245.43
WHEN Q = 88 UNITS	47.0	.1	4624.80	82.95	5.86	4713.61	184293.61
WHEN Q = 89 UNITS	47.5	.1	4674.00	82.02	5.79	4761.81	184341.81
WHEN Q = 90 UNITS	48.0	.1	4723.20	81.11	5.73	4810.04	184390.04
WHEN Q = 91 UNITS	48.5	.1	4772.40	80.22	5.66	4858.28	184438.28
WHEN Q = 92 UNITS	49.0	.1	4821.60	79.35	5.60	4906.55	184486.55
WHEN Q = 93 UNITS	49.5	.1	4870.80	78.49	5.54	4954.84	184534.84
WHEN Q = 94 UNITS	50.0	.1	4920.00	77.66	5.48	5003.14	184583.14
WHEN Q = 95 UNITS	50.5	.1	4969.20	76.84	5.43	5051.47	184631.47
WHEN Q = 96 UNITS	51.0	.1	5018.40	76.04	5.37	5099.81	184679.81
WHEN Q = 97 UNITS	51.5	.1	5067.60	75.26	5.31	5148.17	184728.17
WHEN Q = 98 UNITS	52.0	.1	5116.80	74.49	5.26	5196.55	184776.55
WHEN Q = 99 UNITS	52.5	.1	5166.00	73.74	5.21	5244.94	184824.94
WHEN Q = 100 UNITS	53.0	.1	5215.20	73.00	5.15	5293.35	184873.35
WHEN Q = 101 UNITS	53.5	.1	5264.40	72.28	5.10	5341.78	184921.78
WHEN Q = 102 UNITS	54.0	.1	5313.60	71.57	5.05	5390.22	184970.22
WHEN Q = 103 UNITS	54.5	.1	5362.80	70.87	5.00	5438.68	185018.68
WHEN Q = 104 UNITS	55.0	.1	5412.00	70.19	4.96	5487.15	185067.15
WHEN Q = 105 UNITS	55.5	.1	5461.20	69.52	4.91	5535.63	185115.63
WHEN Q = 106 UNITS	56.0	.1	5510.40	68.87	4.86	5584.13	185164.13
WHEN Q = 107 UNITS	56.5	.1	5559.60	68.22	4.82	5632.64	185212.64
WHEN Q = 108 UNITS	57.0	.1	5608.80	67.59	4.77	5681.16	185261.16
WHEN Q = 109 UNITS	57.5	.1	5658.00	66.97	4.73	5729.70	185309.70
WHEN Q = 110 UNITS	58.0	.1	5707.20	66.36	4.69	5778.25	185358.25

(Continued)

Table 4-3 (Continued)

WITH REORDER POINT SET AT 6 UNITS

	AVERAGE INVENTORY	ANNUAL SHORTAGE	AHC	AOC	ASC	TAC	TAC INCLUDING MATERIALS COST
WHEN Q = 84 UNITS	46.0	.0	4526.40	86.90	1.60	4614.90	184194.90
WHEN Q = 85 UNITS	46.5	.0	4575.60	85.88	1.58	4663.06	184243.06
WHEN Q = 86 UNITS	47.0	.0	4624.80	84.88	1.56	4711.25	184291.25
WHEN Q = 87 UNITS	47.5	.0	4674.00	83.91	1.54	4759.45	184339.45
WHEN Q = 88 UNITS	48.0	.0	4723.20	82.95	1.53	4807.68	184387.68
WHEN Q = 89 UNITS	48.5	.0	4772.40	82.02	1.51	4855.93	184435.93
WHEN Q = 90 UNITS	49.0	.0	4821.60	81.11	1.49	4904.20	184484.20
WHEN Q = 91 UNITS	49.5	.0	4870.80	80.22	1.48	4952.50	184532.50
WHEN Q = 92 UNITS	5C.0	.0	4920.00	79.35	1.46	5000.81	184580.81
WHEN Q = 93 UNITS	5C.5	.0	4969.20	78.49	1.44	5049.14	184629.14
WHEN Q = 94 UNITS	51.0	.0	5018.40	77.66	1.43	5097.49	184677.49
WHEN Q = 95 UNITS	51.5	.0	5067.60	76.84	1.41	5145.86	184725.86
WHEN Q = 96 UNITS	52.0	.0	5116.80	76.04	1.40	5194.24	184774.24
WHEN Q = 97 UNITS	52.5	.0	5166.00	75.26	1.38	5242.64	184822.64
WHEN Q = 98 UNITS	53.0	.0	5215.20	74.49	1.37	5291.06	184871.06
WHEN Q = 99 UNITS	53.5	.0	5264.40	73.74	1.36	5339.49	184919.49
WHEN Q = 100 UNITS	54.0	.0	5313.60	73.00	1.34	5387.94	184967.94
WHEN Q = 101 UNITS	54.5	.0	5362.80	72.28	1.33	5436.41	185016.41
WHEN Q = 102 UNITS	55.0	.0	5412.00	71.57	1.32	5484.89	185064.89
WHEN Q = 103 UNITS	55.5	.0	5461.20	70.87	1.30	5533.38	185113.38
WHEN Q = 104 UNITS	56.0	.0	5510.40	70.19	1.29	5581.88	185161.88
WHEN Q = 105 UNITS	56.5	.0	5559.60	69.52	1.28	5630.40	185210.40
WHEN Q = 106 UNITS	57.0	.0	5608.80	68.87	1.27	5678.94	185258.94
WHEN Q = 107 UNITS	57.5	.0	5658.00	68.22	1.26	5727.48	185307.48
WHEN Q = 108 UNITS	58.0	.0	5707.20	67.59	1.24	5776.04	185356.04
WHEN Q = 109 UNITS	58.5	.0	5756.40	66.97	1.23	5824.60	185404.60
WHEN Q = 110 UNITS	59.0	.0	5805.60	66.36	1.22	5873.18	185453.18

(Continued)

Table 4-3 (Continued)

WITH REORDER POINT SET AT 7 UNITS

	AVERAGE INVENTORY	ANNUAL SHORTAGE	AHC	AOC	ASC	TAC	TAC INCLUDING MATERIALS COST
WHEN Q = 84 UNITS	47.0	.0	4624.80	86.90	.36	4712.07	184292.07
WHEN Q = 85 UNITS	47.5	.0	4674.00	85.88	.36	4760.24	184340.24
WHEN Q = 86 UNITS	48.0	.0	4723.20	84.88	.36	4808.44	184388.44
WHEN Q = 87 UNITS	48.5	.0	4772.40	83.91	.35	4856.66	184436.66
WHEN Q = 88 UNITS	49.0	.0	4821.60	82.95	.35	4904.90	184484.90
WHEN Q = 89 UNITS	49.5	.0	4870.80	82.02	.34	4953.17	184533.17
WHEN Q = 90 UNITS	50.0	.0	4920.00	81.11	.34	5001.45	184581.45
WHEN Q = 91 UNITS	50.5	.0	4969.20	80.22	.34	5049.76	184629.76
WHEN Q = 92 UNITS	51.0	.0	5018.40	79.35	.33	5098.08	184678.08
WHEN Q = 93 UNITS	51.5	.0	5067.60	78.49	.33	5146.42	184726.42
WHEN Q = 94 UNITS	52.0	.0	5116.80	77.66	.33	5194.79	184774.79
WHEN Q = 95 UNITS	52.5	.0	5166.00	76.84	.32	5243.16	184823.16
WHEN Q = 96 UNITS	53.0	.0	5215.20	76.04	.32	5291.56	184871.56
WHEN Q = 97 UNITS	53.5	.0	5264.40	75.26	.32	5339.97	184919.97
WHEN Q = 98 UNITS	54.0	.0	5313.60	74.49	.31	5388.40	184968.40
WHEN Q = 99 UNITS	54.5	.0	5362.80	73.74	.31	5436.85	185016.85
WHEN Q = 100 UNITS	55.0	.0	5412.00	73.00	.31	5485.31	185065.31
WHEN Q = 101 UNITS	55.5	.0	5461.20	72.28	.30	5533.78	185113.78
WHEN Q = 102 UNITS	56.0	.0	5510.40	71.57	.30	5582.27	185162.27
WHEN Q = 103 UNITS	56.5	.0	5559.60	70.87	.30	5630.77	185210.77
WHEN Q = 104 UNITS	57.0	.0	5608.80	70.19	.29	5679.29	185259.29
WHEN Q = 105 UNITS	57.5	.0	5658.00	69.52	.29	5727.82	185307.82
WHEN Q = 106 UNITS	58.0	.0	5707.20	68.87	.29	5776.36	185356.36
WHEN Q = 107 UNITS	58.5	.0	5756.40	68.22	.29	5824.91	185404.91
WHEN Q = 108 UNITS	59.0	.0	5805.60	67.59	.28	5873.48	185453.48
WHEN Q = 109 UNITS	59.5	.0	5854.80	66.97	.28	5922.05	185502.05
WHEN Q = 110 UNITS	60.0	.0	5904.00	66.36	.28	5970.64	185550.64

(Continued)

Table 4-3 (Continued)

WITH REORDER POINT SET AT 8 UNITS

	AVERAGE INVENTORY	ANNUAL SHORTAGE	AHC	AOC	ASC	TAC	TAC INCLUDING MATERIALS COST
WHEN Q = 84 UNITS	48.0	.0	4723.20	86.90	.05	4810.16	184390.16
WHEN Q = 85 UNITS	48.5	.0	4772.40	85.88	.05	4858.33	184438.33
WHEN Q = 86 UNITS	49.0	.0	4821.60	84.88	.05	4906.53	184486.53
WHEN Q = 87 UNITS	49.5	.0	4870.80	83.91	.05	4954.76	184534.76
WHEN Q = 88 UNITS	50.0	.0	4920.00	82.95	.05	5003.00	184583.00
WHEN Q = 89 UNITS	50.5	.0	4969.20	82.02	.05	5051.27	184631.27
WHEN Q = 90 UNITS	51.0	.0	5018.40	81.11	.05	5099.56	184679.56
WHEN Q = 91 UNITS	51.5	.0	5067.60	80.22	.05	5147.87	184727.87
WHEN Q = 92 UNITS	52.0	.0	5116.80	79.35	.05	5196.20	184776.20
WHEN Q = 93 UNITS	52.5	.0	5166.00	78.49	.05	5244.54	184824.54
WHEN Q = 94 UNITS	53.0	.0	5215.20	77.66	.05	5292.91	184872.91
WHEN Q = 95 UNITS	53.5	.0	5264.40	76.84	.05	5341.29	184921.29
WHEN Q = 96 UNITS	54.0	.0	5313.60	76.04	.05	5389.69	184969.69
WHEN Q = 97 UNITS	54.5	.0	5362.80	75.26	.05	5438.10	185018.10
WHEN Q = 98 UNITS	55.0	.0	5412.00	74.49	.04	5486.53	185066.53
WHEN Q = 99 UNITS	55.5	.0	5461.20	73.74	.04	5534.98	185114.98
WHEN Q = 100 UNITS	56.0	.0	5510.40	73.00	.04	5583.44	185163.44
WHEN Q = 101 UNITS	56.5	.0	5559.60	72.28	.04	5631.92	185211.92
WHEN Q = 102 UNITS	57.0	.0	5608.80	71.57	.04	5680.41	185260.41
WHEN Q = 103 UNITS	57.5	.0	5658.00	70.87	.04	5728.92	185308.92
WHEN Q = 104 UNITS	53.0	.0	5707.20	70.19	.04	5777.43	185357.43
WHEN Q = 105 UNITS	53.5	.0	5756.40	69.52	.04	5825.97	185405.97
WHEN Q = 106 UNITS	59.0	.0	5805.60	68.87	.04	5874.51	185454.51
WHEN Q = 107 UNITS	59.5	.0	5854.80	68.22	.04	5923.07	185503.07
WHEN Q = 108 UNITS	60.0	.0	5904.00	67.59	.04	5971.63	185551.63
WHEN Q = 109 UNITS	60.5	.0	5953.20	66.97	.04	6020.21	185600.21
WHEN Q = 110 UNITS	61.0	.0	6002.40	66.36	.04	6068.80	185648.80

5 forecasting demand

demand as a process

For a number of reasons which will become apparent it is best to think of demand as a "process." When we forecast demand we are making estimates about the character of the demand "process" which is "operating," there in the market.

the mean of the demand process

If we forecast that demand next month will be for 46 units of a particular product we do not expect that demand next month will be exactly 46. However, we do expect that the probability that demand will be larger than 46 is no greater than the probability that it will be smaller than 46. In this sense 46 is our estimate of the average demand we would experience over the long run, assuming that market conditions do not change.

The *average* or *mean* is one of the characteristics of the demand process we are estimating when we forecast demand. There are two other characteristics we estimate, but we will consider them later.

the moving average

One method for estimating the mean of the demand process is the moving average. Suppose our records showed the following demand data for a particular metal product, in hundreds of pounds, during the most recent six months:

Date	Actual demand
Jan.	46
Feb.	54
March	53
April	46
May	58
June	49

We might arrive at a forecast of the mean of this process as follows:

$$\frac{46 + 54 + 53 + 46 + 58 + 49}{6} = 51$$

Suppose demand in July proved to be 54 hundred pounds. (We would have had a *forecast error* of 3 hundred pounds.) Continuing with the moving average method of forecasting, we would then average the demand data for February through July to get our forecast of the mean for August:

$$\frac{54 + 53 + 46 + 58 + 49 + 54}{6} = 52.3$$

If we had reason to believe that the market process within which we were operating was constant and unchanging, it would have been better to get the August forecast by averaging the demand data for January through July:

$$\frac{46 + 54 + 53 + 46 + 58 + 49 + 54}{7} = 51.4$$

As a matter of fact, it would have been better to average *all* past monthly data, if we felt the process was constant. In a similar way, if we had a 6 face die and we wanted to test its quality, we would attach more value to a "forecast" of the quality of the die based on larger samples.

In business we behave as though we think there is some element of constancy in demand from period to period. If demand were wholly erratic, without any orderliness whatever, business would be impossible. Since we do business, presumably we feel there is an element of continuity from period to period and that the future is not completely uncertain.

In any kind of forecasting system we try to smooth out "random fluctuations" so as to get an estimate of the mean of the underlying process. At the same time, however, we like our forecasting system to respond to changes in the demand process. We get more smoothing of random fluctuations with a large sample (demand data for a large number of months) but we get better change response with a small sample. The choice of the number of months of demand data to employ is, therefore, crucial.

If we could know somehow what our best sample size was, the moving average is still not the best method for forecasting, as we shall see now.

exponential smoothing

In the moving average, old demand data get the same weight in our average as recent data. Refer again to our original demand data for January through June. The moving average was determined as follows:

$$\frac{46 + 54 + 53 + 46 + 58 + 49}{6} = 51$$

This might have been written:

$$\frac{1}{6}(46) + \frac{1}{6}(54) + \frac{1}{6}(53) + \frac{1}{6}(46) + \frac{1}{6}(58) + \frac{1}{6}(49) = 51$$

Each demand datum received a weight of $\frac{1}{6}$. Notice that we are a bit inconsistent: if we employ only 6 data in determining our moving average—rather than all past data at our disposal—we are demonstrating our conviction that the process is changing. If the process *is* changing—demand is increasing perhaps—then more recent data deserve more weight than older data. Why, then, should we give our most recent month's demand the same weight as the remotest month's demand?

Exponential smoothing is an averaging process which gives more recent data a heavier weight. In exponential smoothing the new forecast, each period, is determined by adjusting the old forecast by a fraction of the forecast error.

For example, in the hypothetical case we've been considering, in June we forecast a demand of 51 for July. In July, however, 54 hundred pounds were demanded. Our forecast error was 3 (that is, we fell *short* by 3 hundred pounds). Using exponential smoothing we would arrive at our forecast for August by adding to our July forecast some fractional part of our forecast error in July. Let us assume that the fractional part is to be 3/10:

Forecast for August = forecast for July + 0.3 (forecast error in July)

or:

Forecast for August = $51 + .3(54\text{-}51) = 51.9$

In an exponential smoothing system, data are given weights in inverse proportion to their *age;* that is, older data get less weight and more recent data get more weight.

In our example above, where we adjusted our forecast by .3 of the forecast error, the four most recent data would get weights as follows:

Table 5-1

	Weight
Current month's demand	0.3
Demand 1 month ago	0.21
Demand 2 months ago	0.147
Demand 3 months ago	0.103
Demand 4 months ago	0.072

The amount of weighting that more recent data get, relative to older data, depends on the fraction we apply to the forecast error. This fraction is called the *smoothing constant* and is usually labeled α. In our example above $\alpha = .3$.

Some notion of the significance of smoothing constants of varying magnitudes can be gained from a comparison of a variety of smoothing constants and the number of demand data which, in a moving average forecasting system, would give somewhat comparable results. In Table 5-1 are shown such comparisons.

Table 5-1

Smoothing constant (α)	Approximate number of data in a moving average
.05	39
.10	19
.15	12
.20	9
.25	7
.30	5.7
.35	4.7
.40	4
.45	3.4
.50	3

Since we are likely to distrust a sample of only 3 or 4 data we find ourselves, in most forecasting systems, using smoothing constants in the range:

$$.05 \leq \alpha \leq .40$$

Thus far we've concerned ourselves with estimating only one of the characteristics of the market process we are experiencing—the mean of the process. Our forecast, each period, is our "smoothed exponential mean" estimate. Henceforth let's refer to it as the SEM, and we can write:

$$SEM_{new} = SEM_{old} + \alpha \left[\begin{array}{c} Actual \\ Demand \end{array} - SEM_{old} \right]$$

Since each new forecast (i.e., each new SEM) is the old forecast plus a fraction of the forecast error, we must have an SEM to begin with. Where some forecasting system other than exponential smoothing has been employed before, on converting to exponential smoothing one might use the most recent forecast as the initial value for SEM_{old}.

In Table 5-2 are running forecasts for January through July, assuming a smoothing constant of 0.3, and assuming that in December our forecast for January was 51.0, and using the data for actual demand which we have employed thus far in our hypothetical case.

Table 5-2

	SEM	Actual Demand	Forecast error
Dec.	51.0	....	....
Jan.	49.5	46	-5.0
Feb.	48.4	54	4.5
March	49.6	53	4.6
April	50.6	46	-3.3
May	49.2	58	7.4
June	51.8	49	-0.2
July	52.5	54	2.2

It is sometimes more convenient to use our forecasting model in the form:

$$SEM_{new} = \alpha \left[\begin{array}{c} Actual \\ Demand \end{array} \right] + \left[1 - \alpha \right] SEM_{old}$$

tracking

One advantage in exponential smoothing has been pointed out: recent data get more weight than older data. A second advantage is that we don't have to retain a string of past data to get new forecasts. Each new value for SEM calls into play only the most recent forecast, the current actual demand and the smoothing constant.

However, we are not prepared to discard all other data as we go from period to period. We are especially interested in the *cumulative sum of the forecast errors* as we go from period to period.

We argued initially, in this chapter, that when we arrive at a forecast, we believe that the probability of a demand in the coming period greater than our forecast is the same as the probability of a demand less than our forecast.

If the process we are estimating is a constant process, then we should expect that over time we would overestimate demand about as much as we underestimate it and therefore that our positive forecast errors would about equal our negative forecast errors and that the cumulative sum of our forecast errors should fluctuate around zero.

In Table 5-2, for example, our forecast errors and their cumulative sum, as we go from period to period, would have been as follows:

	Forecast error	Cumulative sum of the forecast errors
Dec.	....	....
Jan.	-5.0	-5.0
Feb.	4.5	- .5
Mar.	4.6	4.1
Apr.	-3.3	.8
May	7.4	8.2
June	-0.2	8.0
July	2.2	10.2

If we should find that over time the cumulative sum of our forecast errors is growing, then we would deduce that the mean of the demand process is changing and that our forecasts are lagging behind this trend.

Without carrying along with us, from period to period, the cumulative sum of our forecast errors we could not discern trends of this sort.

What action would be appropriate in the face of a positive or negative "build up" in our cumulative sum of the forecast errors? If a build up occurs momentarily, then disappears, it may *not* indicate a trend but only chance variation. If build up persists, however, a trend is possible. If a trend is in fact underway we should want to increase our change response. Before addressing ourselves to the question of when and by how much to adjust the smoothing constant, we should discuss a second characteristic of the process we are estimating when we make a complete forecast.

Knowing the mean of the demand process (or, having a good estimate of it) is not enough for planning purposes. Even if we had reason to believe that the process was stable—that there was no trend —knowledge of the mean alone would be insufficient.

Below are monthly demand data from two different market processes and both have a mean of 48 hundred pounds per month.

	Process 1				Process 2		
	48	hundred	lbs.		26	hundred	lbs.
	45	"	"		0	"	"
	46	"	"		91	"	"
	51	"	"		30	"	"
	48	"	"		110	"	"
	50	"	"		31	"	"
Mean:	48	"	"	Mean:	48	"	"

The difference between the two is, of course, the way they fluctuate. The variation or deviation from the mean in process 1 is small compared to that of process 2. The implications of the difference for reorder point determination are obvious. If lead time were steady at 1 month duration, and if the above were demand during lead time data, with a reorder policy of R = 51, we would have experienced no stockouts with process 1. With process 2, on the other hand, we would have run out of stock during 2 out of the 6 lead time periods, and we would run short a total of 99 hundred pounds.

We need a measure of the variability of demand. One measure would be simply the *average* amount by which the demands in the individual periods differed from the mean of the demand in all the periods.

In process 1 and 2, above, these measures of variability would be as shown in Table 5-3.

Table 5-3

Process 1	Absolute de-[1] viation from the mean	Process 2	Absolute de-[1] viation from the mean
(48 - 48) =	0	(48 - 26) =	22
(48 - 45) =	3	(48 - 0) =	48
(48 - 46) =	2	(91 - 48) =	43
(51 - 48) =	3	(48 - 30) =	18
(48 - 48) =	0	(110 - 48) =	62
(50 - 48) =	2	(48 - 31) =	17
	$\overline{10}$		$\overline{210}$

---

[1] "Absolute" means without regard to whether the datum in an individual period is less than or greater than the mean (i.e., without regard to the sign).

If the total amount of the absolute deviation from the mean in process 1 was 10, the average amount of the absolute deviation *per period* would be 10/6 = 1.67, since there are 6 periods involved. The average amount of the absolute deviation is called the mean absolute deviation, or, the "MAD." The mean absolute deviation for process 2 would be:

$$210/6 = 35$$

The MAD of a process is a convenient measure of its variability. A large MAD means a high degree of variability.

One virtue of the MAD, as a measure of variability, is its simplicity. Another is the ease with which it can be calculated. In spite of these advantages, however, another measure—the *variance*—needs to be included in our inventory policy "equipment." We will examine the variance shortly.

the form of the distribution of a process

We observed at the beginning of this chapter that there are 3 characteristics of the demand process which we should estimate when we forecast. One is the mean of the process; another is the variability of the process; and the third is the *form* of the distribution of the process.

We have already become rather well acquainted with 2 process distributions: the probability distribution for daily demand and the probability distribution for days of lead time, both in Chapter 3.

However, we did not examine the "forms" of those distributions and it is appropriate to do so now.

The probability distribution for demand in our wholesaler's inventory system of Chapter 3 was as follows:

Possible demand per day (units)	Probability
0	.4
1	.3
2	.2
3	.1
	1.0

Our probabilities in a complete (exhaustive) probability distribution always sum to 1.0, meaning that one or another of the events (possible demands listed) is certain to occur.

To get a graphic picture of this distribution let's construct a "histogram" (Figure 5-1).

Figure 5-1

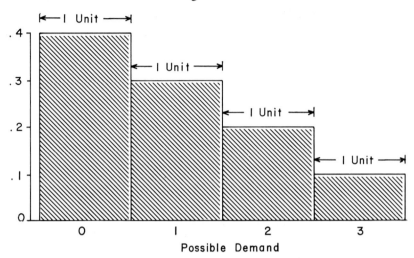

Possible Demand

The height of the box corresponding to a possible demand corresponds to the probability of that demand.

In the histogram of Figure 5-1 we have deliberately drawn each box 1 unit wide, so that the *area* of each box is the *probability* of the event (the demand) it represents. Thus, the left-most box, corresponding to a demand for 0, is 1 unit wide and .4 unit high, yielding an area of .4. Notice that the area under the entire histogram sums to 1:

$$
\begin{aligned}
1 \times .4 &= .4 \\
1 \times .3 &= .3 \\
1 \times .2 &= .2 \\
1 \times .1 &= \underline{.1} \\
& \overline{1.0}
\end{aligned}
$$

Thinking of areas as corresponding to probabilities is useful. The probability of a demand in 1 day *greater than* 0 would be the area under the histogram to the right of the box corresponding to a demand for 0; namely:

$$
\begin{aligned}
& 1 \times .3 \\
+\ & 1 \times .2 \\
+\ & 1 \times .1 \\
& \overline{.6}
\end{aligned}
$$

Let's draw a histogram of our wholesaler's probability distribution for demand during lead time. That distribution was:

Demand during lead time (units)	Probability
0	.1960
1	.2310
2	.2260
3	.1797
4	.0935
5	.0477
6	.0190
7	.0053
8	.0015
9	.0003

Our histogram might appear as shown in Figure 5-2.

Figure 5-2

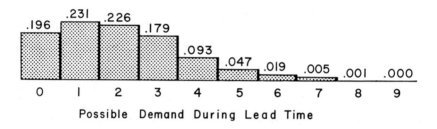

Possible Demand During Lead Time

Once again we've deliberately made the width of each box = 1 unit, so that the area under the histogram = 1.

We could use Figure 5-2 to estimate the probabilities of demand during lead time exceeding certain reorder points, viewing probabilities as corresponding to areas, as before. Figure 5-2 is hard to read, however; so to make it easier let's narrow the widths and raise the heights, as in Figure 5-3.

Our horizontal dimension is now out of proportion to our vertical dimension, but this should not bother us. The area under the curve is 1, and we can get the prbability of a stockout during lead time associated with a reorder point of R = 6, for example, by summing the areas of the boxes corresponding to R = 7, R= 8 and R = 9.

The usefulness of thinking of probabilities as areas will become more apparent if we go further and develop a histogram from some new data.

Demand for 2 x 2 x ¼″ HR angle at the ABC Steel Service Center during the past two years was as shown in Table 5-4.

Figure 5-3

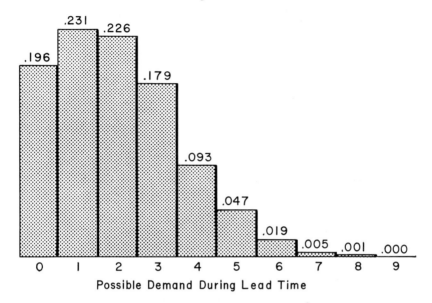

Possible Demand During Lead Time

Table 5-4

	1962			1963		
Jan.	62.4	hundred lbs.		55.2	hundred lbs.	
Feb.	43.1	"		63.2	"	
March	57.7	"		51.5	"	
April	70.5	"		56.1	"	
May	64.1	"		71.4	"	
June	79.1	"		68.4	"	
July	60.8	"		58.4	"	
August	74.8	"		66.2	"	
Sept.	65.6	"		64.8	"	
Oct.	57.6	"		45.8	"	
Nov.	54.3	"		53.5	"	
Dec.	47.1	"		59.7	"	

There does not seem to be any evidence of a trend in the data of Table 5-4. We might, therefore, get some estimate of the probabilities associated with demands of varying magnitudes in the months ahead for the ABC Steel Service Center by constructing a histogram in which areas represent probabilities. Recalling the equivalence of probability and relative frequency, we shall let the *heights* of boxes corresponding to demands in various ranges represent the *frequencies* with which demands in these ranges occurred in the two-year period for which we have data. Referring to Table 5-4 we observe the following frequencies.

Range of demand	Frequency of occurrence	Relative frequency (probability)
40-45	1 time	.04
45-50	2 times	.08
50-55	3 "	.12
55-60	6 "	.25
60-65	5 "	.23
65-70	3 "	.12
70-75	3 "	.12
75-80	1 "	.04
		1.00 approx.

Our histogram would have the form shown in Figure 5-4.

Figure 5-4

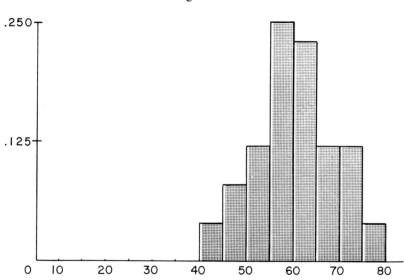

As before, the area under our histogram is 1 if we regard the width of each box as 1; that is, the horizontal distance from 40 to 45 = 1.

Using the histogram of Figure 5-4, and thinking of area as probability, we can find the probability that ABC Steel Service Center will experience a monthly demand greater than, say, 55 hundred pounds, by finding the area under the histogram to the right of the point on the horizontal axis corresponding to 55.

If the histogram in Figure 5-4 represented ABC Company's demand during lead time probability distribution we could, in this way, get at the probability of a stockout during lead time, given any particular reorder point. Equipped as we are with model (3-4), of Chapter 3, we could determine *the optimum reorder point* by this scheme. For example, suppose we employed model (3-4) and found that the optimum probability of a stockout during lead time was:

$$P(DDLT > R) = .16$$

Since a .16 of the area of our histogram in Figure 5-4 lies to the right of a point on the horizontal axis corresponding to 65, our optimum reorder point would be:

$$R = 65 \text{ hundred lbs.}$$

If, however, the optimum probability of a stockout during lead time, from model (3-4), proved to be:

$$P(DDLT > R) = .21$$

Figure 5-5

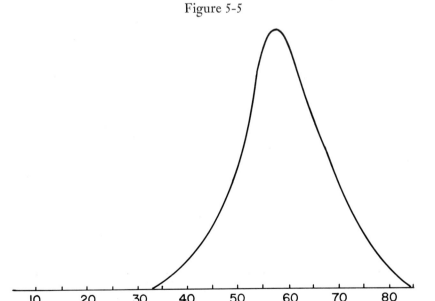

... our histogram is not very helpful. The trouble is that our boxes are too wide, and interpolating "pieces of areas" by splitting boxes vertically is not easy. Why not remedy this difficulty by drawing a smooth curve in place of the step affair in Figure 5-4, such as that in Figure 5-5?

We're not much better off now because finding that point on the horizontal axis to the right of which 21% of the area under the curve lies is somewhat tedious.

We can get around this last problem, however, if we are prepared to assume that the *form* of ABC Company's probability distribution is "normal."

the normal probability distribution

The normal distribution is the well known bell-shaped distribution, samples of which are shown in Figure 5-6.

Figure 5-6

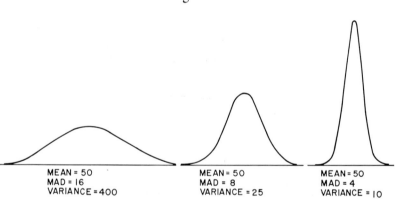

|MEAN = 50|MEAN = 50|MEAN = 50|
MAD = 16 MAD = 8 MAD = 4
VARIANCE = 400 VARIANCE = 25 VARIANCE = 10

Many processes in business can be approximated by some normal distribution. If ABC Company's monthly demand process continued as it has in the two year period for which we have data, and if we observed it over a longer period and finally constructed a histogram with very small ranges (i.e., one box for demand from 40 to 40.05 hundred pounds, etc., rather than one box for demand for 40 to 45 hundred pounds) we might find that ABC Company's demand could be *approximated* by a normal distribution.

The shape of the normal distribution depends on how the MAD or variance compares with its mean, as shown in Figure 5-6. The shape of a particular normal distribution can be *specified* by its mean and its MAD or variance. Therefore the normal distribution which would most clearly approximate ABC Company's demand distribution would be that normal distribution with the same mean and MAD as ABC's. Let us find that normal distribution which best approximates ABC Company's demand process as demonstrated by the 24 months of data we have. First we get the mean:

$$\frac{\begin{aligned}62.4 + 43.1 + 57.7 + 70.5 + 64.1 + 79.1 \\ + 60.8 + 74.8 + 65.6 + 57.6 + 54.3 + 47.1 \\ + 55.2 + 63.2 + 51.5 + 56.1 + 71.4 + 68.4 \\ + 58.4 + 66.2 + 64.8 + 45.8 + 53.5 + 59.7\end{aligned}}{24}$$

$$= 60.5.$$

Recall that the MAD is the Mean of the absolute values of the deviations of individual demand data from the mean of all of the values. Their mean would be:

$$\frac{\begin{aligned}(62.4 - 60.5) + (60.5 - 43.1) + (60.5\ (57.7) \\ + (70.5 - 60.5) + (64.1 - 60.5) + (79.1 - 60.5) \\ + (60.8 - 60.5) + (74.8 - 60.5) + (65.6 - 60.5) \\ + (60.5 - 57.6) + (60.5 - 54.3) \\ + (60.5 - 47.1) + (60.5 - 55.2) + (63.2 - 60.5) \\ + (60.5 - 51.5) + (60.5 - 56.1) + (71.4 - 60.5) \\ + (68.4 - 60.5) + (60.5 - 58.4) + (66.2 - 60.5) \\ + (64.8 - 60.5) + (60.5 - 45.8) + (60.5 - 53.5) \\ + (60.5 - 59.7)\end{aligned}}{24}$$

$$= 7.1.$$

A normal distribution with mean = 60.5 and MAD = 7.1 has the form shown in Figure 5-7.

Obviously the curve of Figure 5-7 and the histogram of ABC Company's demand distribution shown in Figure 5-4 are not the same. Of the two, however, the normal distribution in Figure 5-7 is likely to be a better approximation of the distribution of ABC's demand than the histogram in Figure 5-4, and therefore we are on sounder ground if we base our planning for the future on the curve in Figure 5-7.

Figure 5-7

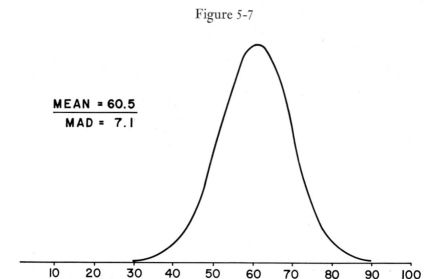

MEAN = 60.5
MAD = 7.1

some properties of the normal distribution

We addressed ourselves to an examination of the normal distribution in our search for a convenient way to determine cumulative probabilities associated with various reorder points. We asked ourselves specifically, "If the histogram of Figure 5-4 represented ABC Company's demand during lead time probability distribution, and if we found from model (3-4) that the optimum probability of a stockout during lead time for ABC Company proved to be:

$$P(DDLT > R) = .21$$

. . . then what would ABC's best reorder point be?"

One of the useful properties of the normal distribution is that the cumulative probabilities associated with any specified *number of multiples* of the MAD above or below the mean *are the same*, regardless of the relationship between the mean and the MAD—i.e., regardless of the "flatness" of the normal curve.

In Table 5-5 are listed a number of multiples of the MAD (and the corresponding number of multiples of *the square root of the variance*) above the mean, and the cumulative probabilities associated with them.

Table 5-5
(Normal Distribution)

(1) Multiples of MAD above the mean	(2) Multiples of $\sqrt{\text{variance above}}$ the mean	(3) Cumulative robability [probability of a value greater than that corresponding to (1) & (2)]
0.000	.000	.500
0.312	.250	.401
0.625	.500	.309
0.937	.750	.227
1.250	1.000	.159
1.560	1.250	.108
1.872	1.500	.070
2.183	1.750	.042
2.500	2.000	.024
2.810	2.250	.013
3.120	2.500	.007

Figure 5-8

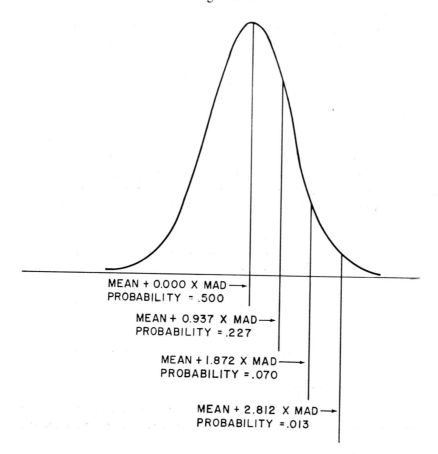

MEAN + 0.000 X MAD →
PROBABILITY = .500

MEAN + 0.937 X MAD →
PROBABILITY = .227

MEAN + 1.872 X MAD →
PROBABILITY = .070

MEAN + 2.812 X MAD →
PROBABILITY = .013

Figure 5-8 makes Table 5-5 more intelligible. Table 5-5 refers to the right half of the normal curve. The area under the entire normal curve = 1. The fractional part of the area to the right of a point corresponding to a specific number of multiples of the MAD (and the corresponding multiples of the $\sqrt{\text{variance}}$) above the mean (to the right of the mean) is listed in Table 5-5. Notice that while half of the area is above (to the right of) the mean, almost all of that half is to the left of a point corresponding to the mean plus 3.12 multiples of the MAD, or to 2.5 multiples of the square root of the variance.

If ABC Company's optimum probability of a stockout during lead time is .21 then ABC Company's optimum reorder point is that point on the normal curve which approximates ABC's demand pattern and which has to the right of it 21% of the area. Referring to Table 5-5, this point is approximately the mean plus .937 multiples of the MAD, or the mean plus .75 multiples of the square root of the variance.

If the mean of ABC's demand during lead time is 60.5 and the MAD = 7.1, then ABC's best reorder point is approximately:

$$\text{Mean} + .937 \text{ x MAD}$$
$$= 60.5 + .937 \text{ x } 7.1$$
$$= 67.15 \text{ hundred lbs.}$$

We will want to return shortly to further use of data such as that shown in Table 5-5 and to see how we can use it more fully in the determination of optimum inventory policy.

We have now examined the three characteristics of the demand process which we estimate when we make demand forecasts:

1. *the mean of the distribution*
2. *the MAD or the variance of the distribution*
3. *the form of the distribution*

Later we will want to examine a form of distribution which, under some circumstances, approximates the demand pattern for most metal products more closely than the normal distribution does. But first we should say a bit more about the MAD and the variance.

forecasting the MAD

In our example of the ABC Steel Service Center we determined MAD by the moving average method; that is, we simply took the average of 24 individual deviations from the mean of all the 24 demand data.

If, as we have argued, exponential smoothing is superior to the moving average method for forecasting the mean, why not use exponential smoothing to forecast MAD?

To forecast MAD by exponential smoothing we would, each period, arrive at a new MAD forecast by adding to the old MAD forecast an amount proportional to the amount by which we missed our previous MAD forecast—paralleling the procedure for forecasting the mean.

Thus our new MAD forecast would be:

$$MAD_{new} = MAD_{old} + \alpha \left[\begin{array}{l} \text{Deviation} \\ \text{Absolute} - MAD_{old} \\ \text{Actual} \end{array} \right]$$

An example will illustrate. Referring to Table 5-4, let's assume it is December, and that we have already forecast that the mean of ABC Company's demand process is 60 hundred pounds and that the MAD is 7 hundred pounds, and that we feel a smoothing constant $\alpha = .2$ gives us the best combination of change response and random fluctuation smoothing.

January's actual demand proves to be 62.4 hundred pounds. Our new forecast, therefore, is:

$$SER_{new} = SEM_{old} + \alpha \left[\begin{array}{l} \text{Actual} \\ \text{Demand} \end{array} - SEM_{old} \right]$$

or:

$$SEM_{new} = 60 + .2 (62.4 - 60) = 60.48$$

The actual absolute deviation of our demand in January from what we forecast was 2.4.

Therefore, our new MAD forecast would be:

$$MAD_{new} = MAD_{old} + \alpha \left[\begin{array}{l} \text{Actual} \\ \text{Absolute} - MAD_{old} \\ \text{Deviation} \end{array} \right]$$

or

$$MAD_{new} = 7 + .2 (2.4 - 7) = 6.1$$

variance and standard deviation

So long as we are prepared to assume that our demand distribution can be approximated by the normal distribution, then the MAD— as a measure of the variability of demand—is suitable. We will find, however, that under some conditions which are common in metals inventory management another distribution—the gamma distribution— gives a better approximation. In dealing with the gamma distribution the variance is a more suitable measure of variability of demand than the MAD, and in dealing with the normal distribution the variance is just as good as the MAD.

The variance of a group of data is the mean of the *squares* of the individual deviations from the mean of the group of data.

We would calculate the variance of the two processes for which we have data in Table 5-3 as follows:

Table 5-5

Process 1	Square of the deviation from the mean	Process 2	Square of the deviation from the mean
$(48 - 48)^2 =$	0	$(48 - 26)^2 =$	484
$(48 - 45)^2 =$	9	$(48 - 0)^2 =$	2304
$(48 - 46)^2 =$	4	$(91 - 48)^2 =$	1849
$(51 - 48)^2 =$	9	$(48 - 30)^2 =$	324
$(48 - 48)^2 =$	0	$(110 - 48)^2 =$	3844
$(50 - 48)^2 =$	4	$(48 - 31)^2 =$	289
	26		6094

Variance = 26/6 = 4.33   Variance = 6094/6 = 1015.67

Sometimes it is more convenient to deal with the standard deviation than with the variance. For *any* distribution the standard deviation is defined as the square root of the variance. For process 1, in Table 5-5, the standard deviation would be $\sqrt{4.33} = 2.08$, and for process 2: standard deviation $= \sqrt{1015.67} = 31.6$

Since the normal distribution is fully specified by either the mean and the MAD, or the mean and the standard deviation, or the mean and the variance, we would expect that the variance, the standard deviation and the MAD bear a constant relationship to one another. The ratio of the MAD to the standard deviation is:

MAD/standard deviation = .8, approximately

... therefore:

$$MAD = .8 \sqrt{Variance}$$

... for the normal distribution.

forecasting the variance

If we choose to employ the variance as our measure of variability, we should forecast the variance from period to period as follows:

$$\text{Variance}_{new} = \text{Variance}_{old} + \alpha \left[\left(\frac{\text{Forecast}}{\text{Error}} \right)^2 - \text{Variance}_{old} \right]$$

As with the MAD, in the normal distribution the cumulative probabilities associated with any specified number of multiples of the $\sqrt{\text{variance}}$ above or below the mean is the same, regardless of the flatness of the normal curve.

Henceforth we will employ the variance as our measure of variability and we will determine our optimum reorder points by employing the optimum cumulative probability model (3-4), and then referring to tables which will tell us the number of multiples of our standard-deviation-during-lead-time forecast above or below our mean-demand-during-lead-time forecast which will yield the optimum probability of a stockout during lead time, and hence will tell us our optimum reorder point.

tracking signal

We observed earlier in this chapter that if the cumulative sum of our forecast errors seems to be getting quite large, then very likely a trend is underway in the process which we are forecasting. What constitutes . . . "getting quite large"?

Clearly if the variance of the process itself is large then large cumulative sums of forecast errors can, at times, be expected as a result of *chance* variations alone, even without a trend.

On the other hand if the variance of the process is small then large cumulative sums of forecast errors most likely indicate a trend. Largeness, then is *relative* and depends on the variance.

A good "tracking signal," designed to tip us off that a significant trend is underway in our demand process—and hence to warn us that it might be appropriate to adopt a larger smoothing constant to get quicker change response—would be some ratio of the cumulative sum of the forecast errors to the $\sqrt{\text{variance}}$. Since we do not *know* the variance of the process the best we can do is use our variance forecast.

We might adopt some rule such as:

"If the ratio of the absolute value of the cumulative sum of the forecast errors to the square root of the variance (i.e., the standard deviation) forecast becomes larger than about 4 or 5, then we should increase our smoothing constant."

In the rule above we specify the *absolute* value of the cumulative sum of the forecast errors because we are interested in increasing the smoothing constant when a trend is underway regardless of whether the trend is up or down.

Setting our tracking signal at about 4 or 5 makes some sense. It develops that in a *normal* process, if the cumulative sum of the forecast errors exceeds (up or down) about 4.6 times the standard deviation, we can have a 95% confidence that a non-random bias (a trend) is present.

In a forecasting system where a tracking signal is employed it is wise to zero out (reduce to zero) the cumulative sum of the forecast errors, and then to return to a lower smoothing constant if the cumulative sum of the forecast errors does *not* grow to the tracking signal again within 2 or 3 forecast periods.

double exponential smoothing

Another strategy for dealing with trends is *double* or *second order* smoothing. Thus far we have dealt with single or first order smoothing. We found that the lag associated with a trend could be detected with a tracking signal and that upon discovering the trend we could increase our smoothing constant to get better change response.

However, if a trend persists, a large smoothing constant will not prevent our forecasts from *lagging* by some amount.

To demonstrate this, observe what happens in Table 5-6. The actual demand data shown have had *all* random fluctuations filtered out of them to make the behavior of our forecasting process more apparent. Notice that demand increases each period by 2 units. Notice further that in spite of our use of a large smoothing constant ($\alpha = .5$) our forecasts continue to lag behind actual demand.

Table 5-6

Period	Forecast ($\alpha = .5$)	Actual demand
1	22	22
2	22	24
3	23	26
4	24.5	28
5	27.3	30
6	28.6	32
7	31.3	34

To deal with this lag we could base our forecast not on single smoothing but on double or second order smoothing. In double smoothing we employ exponential smoothing to smooth our exponentially smoothed forecast:

$$(\text{Double Smoothed Mean})_{new} =$$
$$\alpha(\text{SEM}_{new}) + (1\text{-}\alpha) \, (\text{Double Smoothed Mean})_{old}$$

Just as the new SEM will lag the true mean in a *trend*, the double smoothed mean will lag SEM. Let us now determine our new forecast as follows:

$$\text{New forecast} = 2 \times \text{SEM}_{new} - (\text{Double Smoothed Mean})_{new}$$

The nature of what we are doing becomes apparent if we present this graphically. If all noise were eliminated from the system, then our values for the single smoothed mean and the double smoothed mean would give us two points on what we might assume is our trend line. The difference between twice the value of the single smoothed mean and the double smoothed mean is a third point on this trend line, and constitutes our new forecast for the coming period (see Figure 5-9).

Figure 5-9

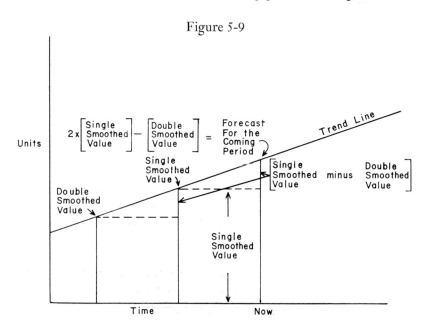

Where the trend involves a constant *rate of change*—thus some constant percentage increase each period rather than some specific number of units increase each period—triple or third order smoothing may be more appropriate.

Some organizations have experimented with forecasting each period a first order, a second order, a third order and even a fourth order estimate and then basing their planning in the current period on the estimate which yielded the smallest forecast error in the previous period.

Where trends are rather sudden and steep, as with many consumer goods, these techniques may be appropriate. In most industrial products their value is questionable.

a practical format for forecasting, using exponential smoothing and a tracking signal

In Table 5-7 is portrayed a format which might be used for forecasting from month to month. Opposite each month are two "rows" of data. In the first row are entered forecast data—the demand forecast and the variance forecast for that month—and the smoothing constant to be employed. In the second row are entered first the demand that actually materialized during that month, followed by the forecast error and the cumulative sum of the forecast errors. At the end of each month we might record actual demand, then calculate the following data:

1. *Forecast error = actual demand — forecast demand*
2. *Cumulative sum of the forecast errors = previous month's cumulative sum of the forecast errors + forecast error for the current month*
3. *Next month's demand forecast = previous month's + α (current month's actual demand — previous month's demand forecast)*
4. *Next month's variance forecast = previous month's variance + α (forecast error)² — previous month's variance forecast*
5. *Tracking signal = absolute value of the cumulative sum of the forecast errors divided by the square root of next month's variance forecast*

If the tracking signal is larger than 4.5 for 3 months in succession we would increase our smoothing constant from 0.1 to 0.25 and zero out the cumulative sum of our forecast errors. If our tracking signal

Table 5-7

	Actual Demand (I)	Forecast Demand (II)	I-II Forecast Error (III)	Variance Forecast (IV)	Cumulative Sum of Forecast Errors (V)	Tracking Signal larger than 4.5? Yes*	No	Smoothing Constant α
Forecast JAN		60.00		256.0			x	0.1
Actual	44.5		-15.5		-15.5			
Forecast FEB		58.5		254.4			x	0.1
Actual	26.6		-31.8		-47.3			
Forecast MARCH		55.3		330.0			x	0.1
Actual	33.1		-22.2		-69.5			
Forecast APRIL		53.1		346.3			x	0.1
Actual	34.2		-18.9		-88.4			
Forecast MAY		51.2		347.5		x		0.1
Actual	18.5		-32.6		-121.0			
Forecast JUNE		47.9		418.5		x		0.1
Actual	76.4		28.5		-92.5			
Forecast JULY		50.7		457.9			x	0.1
Actual	60.7		10.0		-82.5			
Forecast AUG		51.7		422.1			x	0.1
Actual	73.3		21.5		-61.0			
Forecast SEPT		53.9		426.2			x	0.1
Actual	65.2		11.3		-49.7			
Forecast OCT		55.0		396.2			x	0.1
Actual	74.6		19.6		-30.2			
Forecast NOV		57.0		394.8			x	0.1
Actual	74.9		17.9		-12.3			
Forecast DEC		58.8		387.3			x	0.1
Actual	73.7		14.9		2.6			

*If Yes 3 months in succession: 1) Reset Cumulative Sum of forecast errors = 0; and 2) Increase α to 0.25. When Tracking Signal is less than 4.5 for 3 months in succession, return α to 0.1.

remains less than 4.5 for 3 months in succession we would return our smoothing constant to 0.1.

In a computerized record-keeping system the forecasting methodology portrayed in Table 5-7, or a more complex and exhaustive modification of it, could be easily incorporated into the file processing routine by which sales are recorded and master inventory files updated.

Whatever forecasting technique is employed—a computerized technique, a "hand" technique, or some combination of the two—for effective inventory management we require:

1. *A demand forecast*
2. *A variance forecast*

converting a monthly demand and variance forecast into a demand and variance during lead time forecast

In Chapter 3 we assumed that our knowledge of lead time, in our wholesaler's system, was probabilistic. That is, we had a probability distribution for the duration of the lead time period:

Possible lead time (days)	Probability
1	.25
2	.50
3	.25

In this chapter we have dealt with a method for forecasting monthly demand so as to yield a probabilistic estimate. We *could* employ exponential smoothing to forecast the lead time duration so as to yield a probabilistic estimate of that factor. Then, thru simulation —analagous to the drawing of colored balls and the use of random numbers as described in Appendix A—or via analytical means, we could combine these two factors to get a probabilistic estimate of demand during lead time.

However, this can become computationally rather bothersome. We will propose an alternative method which is felt to be satisfactory in metal distribution, particularly where the lead time period is not over 3 or 4 times the forecast interval.

It can be shown that if the forecast interval is one month and the lead time period is LT months, then the mean of the demand during lead time forecast is LT times the mean of the monthly demand forecast, and the variance of the demand during lead time forecast is LT times the variance of the monthly demand forecast. Thus if:

SEM = the mean of the monthly demand forecast
VAR = the variance of the monthly demand forecast
DDLT = the mean of the demand during lead time forecast
V = the variance of the demand during lead time forecast
LT = months of lead time

.... then:

DDLT = SEM x LT
V = VAR x LT

Since our knowledge of the lead time duration is probabilistic, the appropriate strategy would be to select, as a value for LT, the *expected value*. Let us assume, for example, that we feel confident lead time will be between 4 weeks and 8 weeks, and that the weights shown in the left-most column below portray our estimate of the relative likelihoods of the periods shown:

Weight	Possible lead time (weeks)		Probability		
2	4	×	.2	=	.8
2	5	×	.2	=	1.0
3	6	×	.3	=	1.8
2	7	×	.2	=	1.4
1	8	×	.1	=	.8
10			1.0		5.8

If we sum our weights and divide each by the total, we convert them to the probabilities shown in the third column above. Multiplying each possible lead time figure by its probability and summing the products, we arrive at an expected lead time of 5.8 weeks. Dividing 5.8 by 4.3 (the number of weeks in 1 month) we convert our lead time forecast to the same time unit as our demand forecast, and LT $=$ 1.35 months.

seasonality of demand

Where there is an element of significant seasonality in monthly demand, provision should be made for dealing with this factor. This generally involves making an adjustment to the actual demand prior to smoothing, and then an adjustment to the forecast subsequent to smoothing. There is a variety of techniques for dealing with the seasonal factor. However, seasonality in metal products is not, in general, so significant as in many consumer products and methods for dealing with this factor will not be treated here.

In the next chapter we will assume that we have a forecast for one month's demand and the variance associated with it. We will address ourselves to metal products and will employ the models we have developed in previous chapters to learn more about the behavior of metal inventory systems.

6 the metal inventory system

LET'S NOW TAKE INVENTORY of the tools at our disposal for determining optimum policy, and restate the *algorithm* or methodology which we have developed in the previous chapters by addressing ourselves to finding the optimum policy for a particular steel product:

PRODUCT 1: 3" Round, Hot Rolled, OH Annealed Rods

I.   Initial data:
   a. Monthly demand forecast:
   SEM = 36.0 hundred lbs. per month, mean
   VAR = 144.0 hundred lbs. per month, variance
   b. Lead time forecast: 1.4 months
   c. Delivered cost (quantity extra) schedule:*
   Minimum order quantity: 60.0 hundred lbs.

Order quantity	Cost/unit, CPU
60.00 hundred lbs. to 99.99 hundred lbs.	$11.35/hundred lbs.
100.00 hundred lbs. to 199.99 hundred lbs.	11.20/hundred lbs.
200.00 hundred lbs. to 399.99 hundred lbs.	11.15/hundred lbs.
400.00 hundred lbs. and over	11.10/hundred lbs.

   d. Cost estimates:
   Cost of possession, COP = 0.16/year
   Cost of procurement, CPO = $8.00/order
   Stockout cost, SC = $3.70/hundred lbs. short

In the previous chapter we found occasion to use the square root of our variance forecast. To facilitate extracting the square root, a table is provided in Appendix B (Table 1).

In the previous chapter we developed the relationship between a number of multiples of the standard deviation ($\sqrt{\text{Variance}}$) above the mean and the associated cumulative probability for the normal distribution. In Chapter 3 we found how the cumulative probability and the expected stockout during lead time were interrelated. In Table 2 of Appendix B these relationships for the *normal* distribution are summarized in tabular form. The construction of the normal table

---

*This hypothetical quantity extra schedule is used for illustrative purposes only.
II.   Tables 1, 2 and 3

is readily apparent. The left-most column of the table lists values for the cumulative probability, $P(DDLT > R)$. In the second column opposite each value for $P(DDLT > R)$ are the number of multiples, F1, of the standard deviation above the mean which corresponds to these values for the cumulative probability. A reorder point which would yield a stockout-during-lead-time probability of $P(DDLT > R)$ for *any* normal distribution is therefore:

$$R = DDLT + F1 \sqrt{V}$$

.... where:

R = the reorder point
DDLT = the mean of the distribution (our demand during lead time forecast)
V = the variance of the distribution (our variance during lead time forecast)
We found in Chapter 3 how we could determine the expected

stockout during lead time, $E(DDLT > R)$, from a list of the cumulative probabilities associated with a variety of possible reorder points. We found that to determine $E(DDLT > R)$ for a particular reorder point, R, we simply sum the cumulative probabilities associated with R and all reorder points greater than R in our list, and multiply the sum by the increment by which the reorder points in our list differ from each other. The reorder points implied in the first column of Table 1 differ from each other by 25/1000 multiples of the standard deviation.

In the third column of Table 2 are listed—opposite each value for $P(DDLT > R)$—the products of 1) 25/1000, and 2) the sum of the value for $P(DDLT > R)$ under consideration and all those values for $P(DDLT > R)$ smaller than that under consideration. The expected stockout during lead time for a particular value of $P(DDLT > R)$ is therefore:

$$E(DDLT\ R) = F2 \sqrt{V}$$

Instructions for using the tables are repeated at the beginning of Appendix B.
III.   The models we will employ are:

$$Q = \sqrt{\frac{2 \times DPY(CPO + E(DDLT > R) \times SC)}{COP \times CPU}} \qquad (3\text{-}3)$$

$$P(DDLT > R) = \frac{CPU \times COP \times Q}{DPY \times SC + CPU \times COP \times Q} \qquad (3\text{-}4)$$

$$\begin{aligned} TACIM = \ & (DPY/Q) \times E(DDLT > R) \times SC \\ & + (Q/2 + R - DDLT) \times CPU \times COP \\ & + (DPY/Q) \times CPO \\ & + DPY \times CPU \end{aligned} \qquad (4\text{-}1)$$

We begin solving for our optimum policy by calculating: annual demand, DPY; the mean of our demand during lead time forecast, DDLT; and the variance of our demand during lead time forecast, V, and its square root:[1]

DPY = SEM x 12.0 = 36.0 x 12.0 = 432 hundred lbs.
DDLT = SEM x LT = 36.0 x 1.4 = 50.4 hundred lbs.
V = VAR x LT = 144.0 x 1.4 = 201.6 hundred lbs.
$\sqrt{V}$ = 14.2 hundred lbs. (from Table 1, Appendix B)

Next we make an estimate of the optimum order quantity, Q, and select as our value for cost per unit, CPU, that price specified for this order quantity in our delivered price schedule. Let us estimate that the optimum order quantity will fall in the range 60 to 99.99 hundred pounds. CPU, therefore, will be $11.35/hundred pounds.

We now employ models (3-3) and (3-4) *iteratively* to seek an optimal policy which is feasible in the $11.35/hundred pounds price range. We begin by assuming E(DDLT > R) = 0.0. Then, from (3-3):

$$Q = \sqrt{\frac{2 \times 432 \ (8.00 + 0.0 \times 3.70)}{.16 \times 11.35}}$$

$$= 61.6 \text{ hundred lbs.}$$

Now from (3-4):

$$P(DDLT > R) = \frac{11.35 \times 0.16 \times 61.6}{432 \times 3.70 + 11.35 \times 0.16 \times 61.6}$$

$$= 0.07$$

---

[1]The values for the calculated data presented in this sample exercise were obtained by use of a slide rule, and therefore will not have calculator accuracy.

Our next step in the iterative process involves using (3-3) again, but this time with an estimate of E(DDLT > R) better than E(DDLT > R) = 0.0. Factor F2 is required for determining E(DDLT > R) given P(DDLT > R), as indicated in the instruction at the beginning of Appendix B.

Since the ratio $\sqrt{V}/DDLT < 1/2$, we will employ Table 2, the normal table, to get both factors F1 and F2. Turning to Table 2 we find that when P(DDLT > R) = 0.07. F2 = 0.0296. Expected stockout during lead time is therefore:

$$E(DDLT > R) = F2 \times \sqrt{V}$$
$$= 0.0296 \times 14.2 = 0.42 \text{ hundred lbs.}$$

Returning to (3-3):

$$Q = \sqrt{\frac{2 \times 432(8.00 + 0.42 \times 3.70)}{0.16 \times 11.35}}$$

$$= 67.3 \text{ hundred lbs.}$$

Again, from (3-4):

$$P(DDLT > R) = \frac{11.35 \times 0.16 \times 67.3}{432 \times 3.70 + 11.35 \times 0.16 \times 67.3}$$
$$= 0.071$$

Again, from Table 2, factor F2 = .0296, and the expected stockout during lead time is:

$$E(DDLT > R) = 0.296 \times 14.2$$
$$= 0.42 \text{ hundred lbs.}$$

Finally, from (3-3):

$$Q = \sqrt{\frac{2 \times 432(8.00 + 0.43 \times 3.70)}{0.16 \times 11.35}}$$

$$= 67.3 \text{ hundred lbs.}$$

. . . and no further iterations would alter significantly the value for Q.

In calculating this value for the order quantity, Q, we assumed CPU = $11.35/hundred pounds. Since an order quantity in the range

60 to 99.99 hundred pounds *does* cost $11.35/hundred pounds, our
solution is a feasible solution.

Referring again to Table 2, when P(DDLT > R) = 0.071, our
final value for P(DDLT > R) and the one associated with Q = 67.3,
then factor F1 = 1.475. Our best reorder point is therefore (following
the instruction at the beginning of Appendix B):

$$R = DDLT + F1 \times \sqrt{V}$$
$$= 50.4 + 1.475 \times 12.0 = 68.1 \text{ hundred lbs.}$$

What we have done thus far can be summed up with the conclusion: If there were no price break opportunities associated with
order quantities larger than Q = 67.3—that is, if the *base* price were
$11.35/hundred pounds—then our optimum policy would be:

Q = 67.3 hundred lbs.
R = 68.1 hundred lbs.

However, there *are* price breaks associated with larger order quantities, and our next step is to test whether annual material cost saving,
associated with ordering 100 hundred pounds, would be sufficient to
warrant increasing our order quantity.

We begin by calculating our total annual inventory cost including materials cost, associated with Q = 67.3 hundred pounds and
R = 68.1 hundred pounds, using model (4-1):

$$
\begin{aligned}
TACIM &= (432/67.3)0.42(3.70) \\
&+ (67.3/2 + 68.1 - 50.4)11.35(0.16) \\
&+ (432/67.3)8.00 \\
&+ 432 \times 11{:}35 \\
&= \$5054.30 \text{ when: } Q = 67.3, R = 68.1
\end{aligned}
$$

To test whether ordering in lots of 100 hundred pounds would
be advantageous we first determine the optimum reorder point associated with Q = 100.0, using a delivered cost CPU = $11.20/hundred
pounds. From (3-4):

$$P(DDLT > R) = \frac{11.20 \times 0.16 \times 100}{432 \times 3.70 + 11.20 \times 0.16 \times 100}$$
$$= 0.111$$

Again, from Table 2:

$$E(DDLT > R) = 0.0524 \times 14.2$$
$$= 0.744 \text{ hundred pounds}$$

and: $$R = 50.4 + 1.225 \times 14.2$$
$$= 67.8 \text{ hundred pounds.}$$

Form (4-1):

$$TACIM = (432/100.0).744(3.7)$$
$$+ (100.0/2 + 67.8 - 50.4)(11.20)0.16$$
$$+ (432/100.0)8.00$$
$$+ 432 \times 11.20$$
$$= \$5007.46, \text{ when: } Q = 100.0, R = 67.8$$

It pays, therefore, to order in lots of $Q = 100$ rather than 67.3 hundred pounds. However, it may pay to order in lots of $Q = 200$. Proceeding as before, with $Q = 200$ and $CPU = \$11.15/$hundred pounds, from (3-4):

$$P(DDLT > R) = 0.180$$
$$E(DDLT > R) = 1.15 \text{ hundred lbs.}$$
$$R = 61.5 \text{ hundred lbs.}$$
and $TACIM = \$5044.40$, when $Q = 200$, $R = 61.5$ hundred lbs.

Clearly it does not pay to move into a lower per unit cost bracket. Our optimum policy is therefore:

$$Q = 100 \text{ hundred lbs.}$$
$$R = 67.8 \text{ hundred lbs.}$$

The expected annual stockout associated with this policy is:

$$\begin{bmatrix} \text{Expected annual} \\ \text{stockout} \end{bmatrix}$$
$$= E(DDLT > R) \times (\text{No. of lead time periods/year})$$
$$= E(DDLT > R) \times DPY/Q = 0.744 \times 432/100$$
$$= 3.22 \text{ hundred lbs.}$$

Since we expect a demand of 432 hundred pounds in a year we therefore expect to fill $432 - 3.22 = 428.8$ hundred pounds of our year's demand off our own racks. This is an expected service level of:

$$428.8/432 = 99.2\%$$

The expected stockout frequency can be found thus:

With $R = 67.8$, $P(DDLT > R) = 0.111$. If the probability of a stockout during lead time is 0.111, then we expect a stockout every 9 lead time periods. Since we expect $DPY/Q = 432/100 = 4.3$ lead time periods per year, we expect 0.47 stockouts per year, or about 1 every 2 years.

And, finally, the expected annual inventory cost including materials cost associated with our optimum policy is:

$$TACIM = \$5007.46$$

We began by estimating that our optimum policy, ignoring the cost of materials, would be in the order-quantity range corresponding to $CPU = \$11.35$/hundred pounds. It happens that our initial order quantity *did* fall in this price range. If it had not, our initial solution would not have been a feasible solution and we would have been obliged to begin our search again, this time with the appropriate delivered cost figure.

If our initial solution had yielded an order quantity less than 60.00 we would, of course, have based subsequent policy comparisons on $Q = 60.00$ and the best reorder point associated with that order quantity, since the minimum allowable order is 60 hundred pounds.

on passing through the optimum reorder point

What if we implemented this optimum policy for Product 1, and what if the final order prior to the beginning of our reorder period reduced our stock level to 56 hundred pounds? To deal with this situation we might first determine the probability of a stockout during lead time associated with this reorder point. Since:

$$R = DDLT + F1 \times \sqrt{V}$$

... it follows that:

$$
\begin{aligned}
F1 &= (R - DDLT)/\sqrt{V} \\
&= (56.0 - 50.4)/14.2 \\
&= 0.394
\end{aligned}
$$

From Table 2, this value of F1 corresponds most closely to:

$$F2 = 0.2325$$

and therefore: $(EDDLT > R) = 0.2324 \times 14.2$
$$= 3.3 \text{ hundred lbs.}$$

From (3-3) we find:

$$Q = 99.3 \text{ hundred lbs.}$$

... and it would appear we should order $Q = 99.3$ hundred pounds. As before, however, we must ask ourselves if ordering 100, so as to enjoy a materials cost saving, might not be wise. To answer this question we would determine TACIM associated with $Q = 99.3$ and $R = 56.$, and compare this with TACIM associated with $Q = 100$ and $R = 56$. In general it will be found that ordering at less than the optimum re-order point makes larger order quantities appropriate.

behavior of the metal inventory system

To see how growth in demand influences our optimum policy, let us use the methodology we have now demonstrated and see how optimum policy responds to changes in our monthly demand forecast.

Figure 6-1

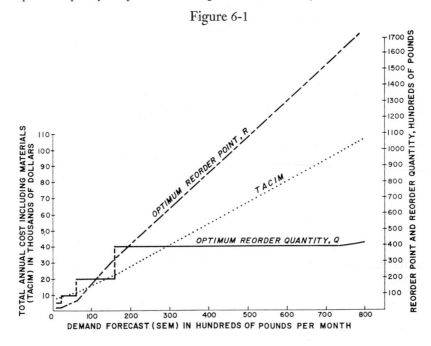

Figure 6-1 shows the behavior of our system as the mean of the monthly demand forecast varies from SEM = 6 hundred pounds through SEM = 800 hundred pounds, with the variance, VAR, being 1/3 of SEM in each case.[2]

It is apparent from Figure 6-1 that the optimum order quantity for Product 1 is either at the minimum allowable order quantity or is at a price break, *until* demand grows to some level beyond the point where buying at the base price is appropriate. The inventory system for Product 1 does not behave precisely as did our wholesaler's model portrayed in Figure 4-1, Chapter 4. This contrast can be attributed to two features of Product 1:

    a. There is a minimum order quantity (60)
    b. The cost of procurement, CPO, is low relative to other costs

Had there been no minimum order quantity the inventory curves pertaining to Product 1 would have behaved more like those portrayed in Figure 4-1, at the lower demand levels.

The influence of the cost of procurement becomes more apparent if we assume that for Product 1 CPO = $20.00 rather than $8.00. The curves of Figure 6-1 would have the form portrayed in Figure 6-2.

It can be seen that as the demand level approaches the point where exploiting the next price break is appropriate there is a region wherein buying in quantities not at the price break is more economical. An ordering cost of CPO = $20.00 is rather high, however. When the cost of procurement is less than CPO = $15.00, and except when demand reaches some level beyond the point where buying at the base price is appropriate, our optimum order quantity, Q, for Product 1, will always be at a price break.

multiple orders outstanding

Notice, in Figure 6-1, that the optimum reorder point is frequently higher than the optimum order quantity. Thus at a forecast demand of SEM = 160 hundred pounds per month the optimum order quantity is Q = 200, and the optimum reorder point is R = 334 hundred pounds.

This would seem to imply that getting our inventory level back above the reorder point, if we ever run out of stock, would be impossible.

---

[2]All data in the *Figures* in this chapter are the result of computer computation, and accuracy can be expected.

Figure 6-2

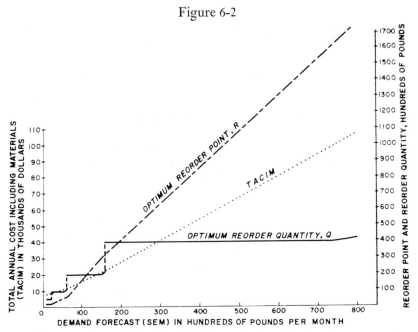

The meaning which should be attached to the optimum reorder point, R, is: R is the optimum quantity *on hand plus on order* at the beginning of the lead time period. That is, "when the sum of the stock on hand and on order drops to R, place an order for Q units."

Suppose, for example, that our monthly demand forecast for Product 1 is SEM = 160.0 hundred pounds. On January 1 we fill a customer's order which reduces our stock level to 330 hundred pounds. Since our optimum reorder point is 334 hundred pounds, we place an order for 200 hundred pounds, our optimum order quantity. We now have "on hand and on order" 330 + 200 = 530 hundred pounds. Prior to the arrival of our replenishment supply 196 hundred pounds more are withdrawn, reducing our supply on hand to 330 − 196 = 134 hundred pounds, on February 1. We now have on hand and on order 134 + 200 = 334 hundred pounds, and we are again at our reorder point. We place another order for 200 hundred pounds, our optimum order quantity, and we now have "on hand and on order" 134 + 200 + 200 = 534 hundred pounds, and we have 2 orders outstanding.

We can gain further insight into the behavior of the inventory system of Product 1 if we plot a curve relating order quantity and total annual cost including materials cost for a number of different demand levels, varying from SEM = 62 thru SEM = 74 hundred pounds with $\sqrt{\text{VAR}}$ of the demand forecast, in each case, equal to 1/3 SEM. (In the curve of figure 6-3, the total annual cost including materials cost is, in each case, based on the optimum reorder point associated with the order quantity shown.)

Figure 6-3

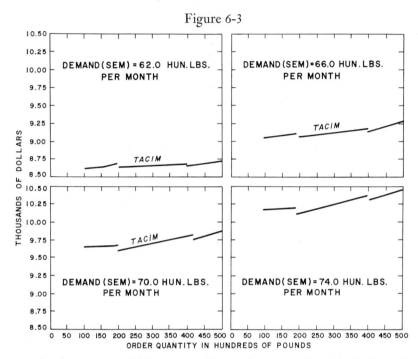

As the curves of Figure 6-3 show, the next price break (i.e., Q = 200.0) becomes progressively more attractive as the monthly demand increases until finally at SEM = 68 hundred pounds buying in quantities of Q = 200 hundred pounds rather than 100 begins to pay.

the gamma tables and high variability in demand

Where the ratio of the standard deviation (i.e., $\sqrt{\text{variance}}$) to the mean of a forecast is smaller than 1/2, the normal distribution can be employed with some confidence. Where this ratio exceeds 1/2, however, the normal distribution becomes suspect. Demand fluctuates rather violently from month to month for many metals products. Where the demand fluctuation is large the ratio of the standard deviation to the mean of the forecast may easily exceed 1/2. Under these conditions we can approximate the process generating our demand with greater confidence by use of the gamma distribution.

Suppose, for example, that monthly demand data for a hypothetical product over the past 2 years was as follows:

	First Year	Second Year
Jan.	0 hundred lbs.	100 hundred lbs.
Feb.	90 hundred lbs.	0 hundred lbs.
Mar.	150 hundred lbs.	0 hundred lbs.
Apr.	0 hundred lbs.	65 hundred lbs.
May	10 hundred lbs.	150 hundred lbs.
June.	0 hundred lbs.	30 hundred lbs.
Jul.	70 hundred lbs.	170 hundred lbs.
Aug.	170 hundred lbs.	45 hundred lbs.
Sept.	20 hundred lbs.	90 hundred lbs.
Oct.	110 hundred lbs.	0 hundred lbs.
Nov.	40 hundred lbs.	80 hundred lbs.
Dec.	280 hundred lbs.	10 hundred lbs.

If we compose a frequency distribution from these data we have the following:

Range of demand	Frequency of occurrence (no. of months)
0 — 60 hundred lbs.	12
60 — 120 hundred lbs.	7
120 — 180 hundred lbs.	4
240 — 300 hundred lbs.	1

In Figure 6-4 is a histogram drawn from this frequency distribution.

The mean monthly demand in this example proves to be 60.8 hundred pounds, and the variance is 5,240 hundred pounds. If we were to forecast lead time at 1 month, and if we were to employ the normal distribution as an approximation of the histogram of Figure 6-4, we would base our policy determination on the normal distribution with mean = 60.8, variance = 5240 and $\sqrt{\text{variance}}$ = 72.4. Recall from Table 5-5, however, that 15.9% of the normal distrbiution lies above the mean plus 1 multiple of the $\sqrt{\text{variance}}$. Now, since the normal distribution is a *symmetrical* distribution, clearly 15.9% of the normal distribution lies *below* the mean *minus* 1 multiple of the $\sqrt{\text{variance}}$. This means that if we employ the normal distribution as an approximation of the histogram of Figure 6-4, then we are assuming that 15.9% of our distribution lies below the point:

$$\text{mean} - 1 \times \sqrt{\text{variance}} = 60.8 - 72.4 = -11.6$$

This means we are assuming that 15.9% of our lead time periods we expect to have a demand for *less* than −11.6 hundred pounds. We do

Figure 6-4

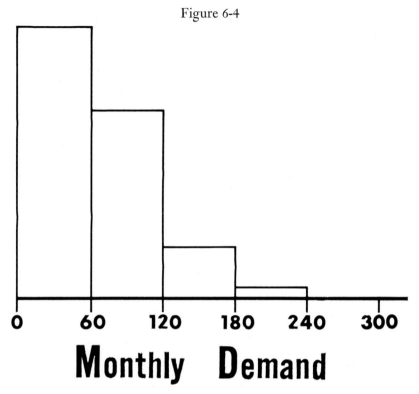

0   60   120   180   240   300

Monthly Demand

not sell less than zero units! Clearly the normal distribution is *not* a good approximation of our histogram of Figure 6-4.

In contrast to this, one of a family of gamma distributions (another theoretical distribution) will approximate our histogram of Figure 6-4 rather accurately. In Figure 6-5 the gamma with mean $= 60.8$ and $\sqrt{\text{variance}} = 72.4$ is superimposed on the histogram of Figure 6-4. The quality of the "fit" is apparent.

To repeat: when the ratio $\sqrt{\text{variance}}/\text{mean}$ is less than or equal to $\frac{1}{2}$ we will find the normal distribution is suitable, and since it is less involved than the gamma distribution we should use it. When this ratio is greater than $\frac{1}{2}$, however, the normal distribution will give us unrealistic answers, leading to sub-optimal policies, and we should employ tables based on the gamma distribution in spite of its somewhat greater complexity.

Table 3 of Appendix B consists of a number of tables each the product of the gamma distribution. Their use parallels that of the normal distribution somewhat, and explicit instructions for using the gamma tables are presented at the beginning of Appendix B.

Figure 6-5

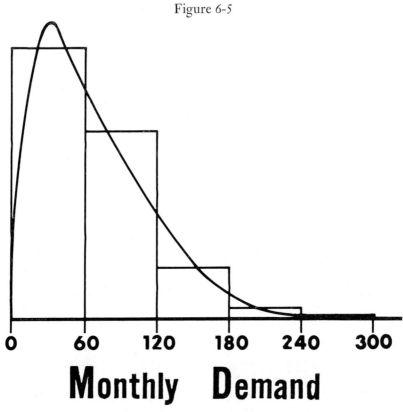

| 0 | 60 | 120 | 180 | 240 | 300 |

Monthly Demand

    The first step for determining optimum policy in our algorithm is to find the ratio of the $\sqrt{\text{variance}}$ and the mean of the demand during lead time forecast, and to choose the table most appropriate for that ratio.

    We can perceive more about the behavior of our metals inventory system if we allow the $\sqrt{\text{variance}}$ of our demand forecast to increase, while keeping the mean of that forecast constant. Returning to our original forecast of demand for Product 1 (i.e., DDLT = 50.4 hundred pounds/month) let us let the standard deviation of that forecast vary from 15 hundred pounds through 75 hundred pounds. If we determine the optimum policy for Product 1 as the standard deviation varies in this fashion—using the gamma tables when appropriate—we will get the results tabulated in Table 6-1. It is apparent, as we should expect, that as the variability of demand increases, the optimum reorder point increases. Meeting demand becomes increasingly expensive, however, and the service level associated with the optimum policy progressively decreases. Profit would also suffer since the total annual cost, TACIM, would increase while demand remains constant at 36 hundred pounds per month.

The behavior of Product 1 as portrayed by Figures 6-1, 6-2 and 6-3 is typical of metals in general. This being the case an opportunity to simplify our algorithm must immediately occur to us.

In the iterative calculations which yielded our optimum policy for Product 1 when monthly demand was forecast at SEM $= 36$ hundred pounds, we busied ourselves entirely in the range of order quantities wherein our optimum order quantity was sure to be at a price break. That is, ordering at the base price was out of the question.

Table 6-1*

$\sqrt{\text{Variance}}$ (standard deviation)	$\sqrt{\text{Variance}}$ DDLT	Table employed	Optimum reorder point, R	Service level
15 hundred pounds	.29	NORMAL	68 hundred pounds	99.8%
30 hundred pounds	.59	GAMMA	87 hundred pounds	97.2%
45 hundred pounds	.89	GAMMA	89 hundred pounds	96.0%
60 hundred pounds	1.19	GAMMA	124 hundred pounds	93.0%
75 hundred pounds	1.48	GAMMA	130 hundred pounds	90.2%

Since buying in order quantities less than minimum order quantity required for base price involves us in a choice of order quantities associated with price breaks—only a small number of possible alternative choices—might it not be possible to determine our optimum order quantity prior to and independently of the reorder point? If this could be done without introducing serious inaccuracies in our optimum policy-determining strategy, it would seem to be well justified: we could avoid the bulk of the computation involved in applying our algorithm to individual metal products.

We have already observed that during our iterative process Q and R do not interact intimately. This should further suggest that we might in fact, determine Q before and independently of R.

If we can develop a method for doing this it will not make our iterative process involving models (3-3) and (3-4) wholly unnecessary. Any time we find that demand is adequate to warrant buying at the base price we will be obliged to fall back on our more time-consuming iterative process to find that optimum combination of Q and R, as was done to find the optimum policies represented by that segment of the curves of Figure 6-1 corresponding to demands in excess of SEM $= 738$ hundred pounds/month.

---

*Calculations to slide rule accuracy.

the two-bin inventory system

If we ignore R in estimating the optimum order quantity we are basing our decision-making on a "two-bin" inventory system analysis. We might *imagine* that we have two different inventory bins for each product. Normally we meet demand out of bin 1, the order quantity bin. Except during lead time bin 2 has in it a supply of stock equal to our optimum reorder point, R. When the inventory level in bin 1 drops to 0, we place a replenishment order for Q units and begin meeting our demand out of bin 2 during the lead time period.

In the two-bin inventory system we manage the bins somewhat independently of each other. Specifically, we find the optimum order quantity (the maximum inventory level in bin 1) by "balancing" annual holding cost and the annual cost of materials, ignoring the influence of the reorder point on either. Then, having determined the optimum order quantity for bin 1, we employ this order quantity, using model (3-4), to determine the optimum reorder point (the maximum inventory level for bin 2).

In the next chapter we address ourselves to means for managing bin 1.

7

optimum order quantity for a given annual demand, cost of possession, ordering cost, and quantity extra schedule

IN THIS CHAPTER WE WILL build upon many of the concepts and principles developed in previous chapters to develop a means of determining the maximum inventory level in "bin 1" of a two-bin inventory system. This maximum level, Q, is the optimum order quantity which will result in the minimization of the sum of the following costs:

1. *Annual holding cost, AHC*
2. *Annual ordering cost, AOC*
3. *Annual materials cost, AMC*

Or:

$$\text{TACIM} = Q/2 \text{ x CPU x COP} \\ + (\text{DPY}/Q) \text{ x CPO} \\ + \text{DPY x CPU}$$

It will be noted that this TACIM differs from model (4-1) in two respects:

1. *The holding costs for material in "bin 2" have not been included.*
2. *The annual stockout costs are not included.*

Each of these factors is related to the determination of the optimum reorder point, R, which determines the level of stock in "bin 2." Since we are presently addressing ourselves only to the determination of the optimum order quantity, Q, the "maximum inventory level in bin 1," we will not consider the interrelationship between Q and R in determining the "bin 1" level.

141

order quantity formula

By way of review, it will be recalled that in Chapter 2 the "classic" EOQ formula was developed. When dealing only with bin 1, as would be appropriate under a condition of certainty, the Q which minimized TAC was as follows:

$$Q = \sqrt{\frac{2 \times \text{DPY} \times \text{CPO}}{\text{CPU} \times \text{COP}}}$$

By plugging the pertinent data and costs into this formula we obtain an "answer." This would reliably provide us with an optimum Q were it not for the factors of *minimum order quantities* and *quantity* extras schedules. The problem is that the Q we obtain may be for *less* than the minimum order quantity; in addition, we must be prepared to answer the question: Would not our *TACIM* be less if we purchased our material in a larger order-quantity bracket? These factors may be illustrated by looking at a specific example. Assume the following data.

1. *Estimated DPY of 100 hundred pounds*
2. *COP = 12% per year*
3. *CPO = $4.00 per order*
4. *CPU = $8.00 per hundred pounds, at base cost*
5. *Quantity extra schedule:*

```
60 to  99.99 hundred pounds, base plus $ .35/100 lbs.
100 to 199.99 hundred pounds, base plus $ .15/100 lbs.
200 to 399.99 hundred pounds, base plus $ .05/100 lbs.
400 hundred pounds or over, base price of $8.00/100 lbs.
```

6. *Minimum purchase quantity is 60 hundred pounds.*

Making use of this data in our order quantity formul results in a Q of 28.86 hundred pounds; i.e.,

$$Q = \sqrt{\frac{2 \times 100.0 \times \$4.00}{.12 \times \$8.00}} = 28.86 \text{ hundred pounds}$$

If we could purchase 28.86 hundred pounds at the *base price* of $8.00 per hundred pounds, then we could use this Q for our "optimum" order quantity, knowing that it reflected the minimum point on a relevant total cost curve. However, we are restricted to a minimum purchase of 60 hundred pounds, and base price is only available with a Q of 400 hundred pounds or greater.

A further move might be to recalculate Q using the unit cost of $8.35 per hundred pounds, the applicable price when purchasing in the minimum purchase quantity of 60 hundred pounds. This does not solve our problem, however, since this calculation results in a Q of 28.25 hundred pounds, a quantity even further away from the minimum purchase quantity of 60 hundred pounds.

use of total annual inventory cost, including materials

One way out of our dilemma is to fall back on model (4-1). For example, in our present illustration we already know that Q is lower than our minimum order quantity of 60 hundred pounds. This means that we will be required to purchase in *at least* an order quantity of 60 hundred pounds, with TACIM as follows:

$$\text{TACIM} = \text{AHC} + \text{AOC} + \text{AMC}$$
$$\text{AHC} = 60.0/2 \text{ x } \$8.35 \text{ x } .12 = \$ 30.06$$
$$\text{AOC} = 100./60. \text{ x } \$4.00 \qquad = \$ 6.68$$
$$\text{AMC} = 100. \text{ x } \$8.35 \qquad\quad = \$835.00$$
$$\text{TACIM} = \overline{\$871.74}$$

Note that the annual holding cost exceeds the annual ordering cost; that is, we are *beyond* the point where annual ordering cost equals annual holding cost. We may now make use of an important principle enunciated in Chapter 4, which was stated as follows:

> In real inventory systems, *once we've passed the point where ordering cost equals annual holding cost* the slope of our total annual cost curve is always upward toward the right. This means that if there is an advantage in ordering in quantities larger than the order quantity corresponding to the point where these two curves cross, *the best order quantity will always be at a price break*

Making use of this principle, then, we could determine TACIM when purchasing our material in quantities of either 60, 100, 200 or 400 hundred pounds, and then base our Q on that order quantity which resulted in the minimum TACIM. This would still involve some calculation, however, and as we shall soon see, for many classes of metal items there is a means by which tables may be developed which will greatly simplify such calculations.

changes in cost components of TACIM as Q is increased

In our present example it has now been shown that the optimum order quantity, Q, will be either 60, 100, 200, or 400 hundred pounds.

Let us note the changes in the cost components of TACIM when we use a Q of 100 hundred pounds rather than the Q of 60 prevoiusly calculated. With a Q of 100 hundred pounds our material cost will be reduced to $8.15 per hundred pounds, and:

		(Comparative costs when Q = 60.)
AHC = 100./2 × $8.15 × .12 =	$ 48.90	($ 30.06)
AOC = 100./100. × $4.00 =	$ 4.00	($ 6.68)
AMC = 100. × $8.15 =	$815.00	($835.00)
TACIM =	$867.90	($871.74)

In parentheses are shown the corresponding costs when our requirements were met in the 60 hundred pounds purchase-quantity bracket. It is very important to note the direction of the changes in cost components as the order quantity has been increased, since this provides the means by which we may simplify the determination of optimum order quantities. Note that as we move from a Q of 60 to a Q of 100 the annual direct material and annual ordering costs *decrease*, while the annual holding cost *increases*. *Thus*, before buying in a larger order-quantity bracket, where the annual holding costs are increased, it is necessary to make certain that the annual savings in direct material and ordering costs are *at least equal to* the increased holding costs. A further point to note is that the costs which decrease, i.e., AOC and AMC, are a function of the demand per year (DPY). Thus, the greater the DPY the greater will be the savings from buying material in a larger order-quantity bracket. With a high-enough DPY we know that the savings in direct material and ordering costs will outbalance the increased annual holding costs resulting from the large order quantities associated with base-quantity prices. This phenomenon is graphically illustrated in Figures 6-1, 6-2, and 6-3, which indicate how the optimum order quantity increases, by steps, with increasing demand forecasts. Figure 6-3, in particular, shows that the "next higher" price-break order quantity becomes progressively more attractive as the monthly demand increases.

calculation of indifference points

Since the next-higher price-break order quantity becomes progressively more attractive with increased demand, it is apparent that at some given DPY the total annual costs will be the same whether material is purchased, say, in either 60 *or* 100 hundred-pound order quantities. This quantity, in demand per year (or demand per month), is a point of indifference, in that we are "indifferent" to which order quantity we will use, with either order quantity resulting in an equivalent TACIM. The example we have been using will serve as an illustration. What we want to calculate is that point, in demand per year, where the *increased* holding cost from buying in a larger order-quantity bracket *just equals* the *decreased* cost resulting from the lower material and ordering costs resulting from the use of this larger order-quantity bracket. At this level of demand the TACIM when Q = 60 hundred pounds will just equal the TACIM when Q = 100 hundred pounds, or:

$$\text{TACIM}_{Q = 60.} = \text{TACIM}_{Q = 100.} \qquad (7\text{-}1)$$

$$\text{TACIM}_{Q = 60.} =$$
$$(60./2 \text{ x } \$8.35 \text{ x } .12) + (\text{DPY}/60. \text{ x } \$4.) + (\text{DPY x } \$8.35)$$
$$\text{TACIM}_{Q = 100.} =$$
$$(100./2 \text{ x } \$8.15 \text{ x } .12) + (\text{DPY}/100. \text{ x } \$4) + (\text{DPY x } \$8.15)$$

With the above equations equal to one another, we solve for DPY and obtain:

$$\text{DPY} = \frac{(100./2 \text{ x } \$8.15 \text{ x } .12) - (60./2 \text{ x } \$8.35 \text{ x } .12)}{(\$4./60. - \$4./100.) + (\$8.35 - \$8.15)}$$
$$= \frac{\text{Total increased holding costs}}{\text{Ordering and material savings per unit when Q} = 100. \text{ vs. } 60.}$$
$$= 83 \text{ hundred pounds}$$

Hence:

$$\text{TACIM}_{Q = 60.} = (60./2 \text{ x } \$8.35 \text{ x } .12) + (83./60 \text{ x } \$4.) + (83. \text{ x } \$8.35)$$
$$\$728.64 \quad = \quad \$30.06 \quad + \quad \$5.53 \quad + \quad \$693.05$$
$$\text{TACIM}_{Q = 100.} = (100./2 \text{ x } \$8.15 \text{ x } .12) + (83./100. \text{ x } \$4.) + (83. \text{ x } \$8.15)$$
$$\$728.67 \quad = \quad \$48.90 \quad + \quad \$3.32 \quad + \quad \$676.45$$

Thus, with the data and costs as given in our example, we can say that if DPY is *less than* 83 hundred pounds, buy in 60 hundred-pound quantities. If DPY is *greater than* 83 hundred pounds per year, buy in *at least* 100 hundred-pound order quantities. A similar calculation must be made for the point of indifference between 100 and 200 hundred pounds, and between 200 and 400 hundred-pound order quantities.

These calculated points of indifference may then be placed in a table such as is illustrated by Table 7-1.

Table 7-1
Indifference Point Table

Regular-size hot-rolled bars
COP = .12; CPO = $4.00
Quantities in table are hundreds of pounds demanded per year

Base cost per 100 lbs.	Buy 60 hundred pounds to DPY of:	Buy 100 hundred pounds to DPY of:	Buy 200 hundred pounds to DPY of:
$ 7.00	72.5	347.5	1390.
$ 8.00	83.0	397.5	1590.
$ 9.00	93.5	447.5	1790.
$10.00	104.0	497.5	1990.

preparation of indifference point tables

For most classes of metal items it is relatively easy to prepare indifference point tables such as Table 7-1. Only a few calculations are required, and then the tables may be completed by extrapolation. The reason this is possible is because as the base cost increases, the holding costs increase in direct proportion, while the value of the denominator of the indifference point formulae remains unchanged.* Thus, once the incremental difference between the indifference points for base costs of, say, $7.00 and $8.00 per hundred pounds has been determined, this incremental value may be added to the indifference value for $8.00 per hundred pounds of material to get the indifference point for the $9.00 per hundred pounds of material, etc. These relationships may be noted in Table 7-1, where the incremental difference between $7.00 and $8.00 per hundred pounds of material is 10.5, 50, and 200 hundred pounds for the 60, 100, and 200 hundred-pound brackets, respectively. As will be noted, these same differences apply between the $8.00 and $9.00 per hundred pounds brackets. Hence, Table 7-1 may be prepared after calculating only six "indifference" points.

return on invested capital formula

The use of a "return on invested capital" formula provides additional meaning to the indifference points shown in Table 7-1. Assume that a holding cost of 12% per year has been determined to be applicable for a given class of inventory items. Would it not be reasonable to set up some such rule as: Order in minimum order quantities

---

*This is not true with "percentage" quantity extras, which will be discussed shortly.

unless the return on the extra invested capital is *at least* 12%? A formula which could be used to test the rate of return when going to a higher order-quantity bracket, is as follows:

$$\text{Gross percent return on extra invested capital} = \frac{\text{Savings}}{\text{Extra investment}} \times \frac{\text{DPY}}{\text{Q}}$$

Let us test this formula, making use of the following data:

CPO = $4.00
COP = .12
DPY = 83 hundred pounds
CPU = $8.00 per hundred pounds in base cost quantities.

What we want to test, then, is the return on the extra invested capital if this material is purchased in 100 hundred-pound order quantities rather than in 60 hundred-pound minimum order quantities. *Each time* 100 hundred pounds is purchased the direct material savings, at $ .20 per hundred pounds ($8.35 — $8.15), is $20.00. In addition, each time 100 hundred pounds is ordered there is a saving in ordering cost. While it costs $4.00 each time 100 hundred pounds is ordered, it would cost $6.67 (i.e., 100/60 x $4.00) if this same amount of material were ordered 60 hundred pounds at a time. Thus, the ordering cost savings is $2.67, which when added to the $20. savings in direct materials results in a total savings of $22.67 *each time* 100 hundred pounds is ordered. The additional investment in buying 100 hundred pounds over 60 hundred pounds, and basing the average investment on one-half the order quantity (i.e., Q/2), is $157.00. Hence, the savings is $22.67, the additional investment is $157.00, and the factor DPY/Q tells us how many times per year we gain the $22.67 saving. In the original formula:

$$\text{Gross percent return on additional investment} = \frac{\$\,22.67}{\$157.00} \times \frac{83.}{100.} = 12\%$$

It will be recalled that the DPY of 83 hundred pounds was the point of indifference calculated earlier, indicating that at a base cost of $8.00 per hundred pounds, COP of .12, and CPO of $4.00, we could order in 100 hundred-pound order quantities *if* our DPY was 83 hundred pounds or greater. The return on invested capital formula demonstrates that at 83 hundred pounds DPY we *are* getting a 12%

return on our extra investment, just as we would expect. The formula also clearly shows that if our DPY were greater than 83 hundred pounds we would most certainly want to purchase in at least 100 hundred-pound order-quantities, since our return would be proportionately greater than 12%.

points of indifference related to holding-cost percentages

The preceding explanations of the "points of indifference" indicate how these points vary in direct proportion to the holding cost percentage used. The formula, it will be recalled, was:

$$DPY = \frac{\text{Increased holding costs when buying in larger quantity}}{\text{Savings per unit when buying in larger quantity}}$$

As is readily apparent from the formula, the points of indifference are very sensitive to the holding cost percentage, as illustrated in Table 7-2.

Table 7-2

Points of indifference between Q of 60 and Q of 100 hundred pounds
Unit holding cost percentage

Base cost per 100 pounds	6%	10%	12%	16%	20%
$ 7.00	36.2	60.5	72.5	96.6	120.5
8.00	41.5	69.5	83.0	111.0	138.5
9.00	46.8	75.0	93.5	125.0	156.0
10.00	52.2	87.0	104.0	139.0	174.0

In the table it will be noted that with a unit holding cost of as low as 6% we would be guided to start buying 100 hundred pounds of $8.00 per hundred pounds of material when our DPY was as low as 41.5 hundred pounds. When using a 12% holding cost, as was used in our earlier example, we found that we would not start buying in 100 hundred-pound quantities until DPY was 83 hundred pounds. Thus, while our unit holding cost increased from 6% to 12% the DPY point of indifference increased from 41.5 to 83 hundred pounds, or in direct proportion.

This direct proportionality provides a basis for the revision of ordering tables should there be a change in the unit holding cost. For example, suppose that ordering tables had been developed for a unit holding cost percentage of 12%, but that further analysis had shown that 16% was a more accurate holding cost percentage. The new ordering tables could easily be prepared merely by multiplying the DPY figures in the old tables by a factor of 1.33 (i.e., 16%/12%). For example, in the example worked out previously, the point of in-difference was 83 hundred pounds, based upon an order cost of $4., a cost of possession of 12%, and a material cost of $8.00 base per hundred pounds. If the same calculation had been made using a 16% cost of possession the point of indifference would have been 111 hundred pounds (i.e., 83 hundred x 1.33).

other types of order-quantity tables

The foregoing discussion of the method of preparing "ordering tables" will provide the basis for calculating order-quantity tables for a large number of different classes of metals; e.g., hot-rolled bars, cold-rolled bars, alloy bars, hot-rolled and cold-rolled sheets, stainless sheets, carbon plates, etc. A slightly different calculation is required for setting up an order-quality table for items such as structural shapes, for example, for which both the base price and the minimum order quantity are at 40 hundred pounds. Here the regular economic order-quantity formula could be used. *If* the Q from the use of the formula was for less than 40 hundred pounds, then the 40 hundred-pound order-quantity would be used. For convenience, however, an ordering table may be prepared, making use of the formula:

$$Q = \sqrt{\frac{2 \times DPY \times CPO}{COP \times CPU}}$$

Instead of calculating the Q for *each* item, assume that orders will be submitted for quantities such as, say, 40 hundred pounds, 50 hundred pounds, 60 hundred pounds, etc. Hence, these figures are the "Q" in the above formula, and all that remains is to calculate how high DPY must be before one would purchase in these predetermined quantities. Solving the formula for DPY gives:

$$DPY = \frac{Q^2 \times COP \times CPU}{2 \times CPO}$$

Thus, for example, if: CPU = $8.00 per hundred pounds
                          COP = .12 per year
                          CPO = $5.00

Question: What should be the DPY before buying 60 hundred-pound quantities?

$$DPY = \frac{60.^2 \times .12 \times \$8.00}{2 \times \$5.00} = 346 \text{ hundred pounds.}$$

Hence, we would start buying in 60 hundred-pound order quantities only if our DPY was 346 hundred pounds or greater.

percentage quantity extras

Perhaps metal tubing provides the best example of the complexities entering into the determination of optimum order quantities when percentage quantity extras apply. In fact, just the pricing of tubes is a complex matter, as is indicated by the numerous examples of price calculations included in the mill price-schedule books. Because of the manner in which quantity extras and distributor discounts are applied there is no simple relationship between a product base price and final price, before freight, when purchased in the various purchase-quantity brackets. This complexity is best illustrated by an example. Table 7-3 shows the quantity extra and distributor discounts applying to one type of mechanical tubing.

Table 7-3

Quantity—pounds or feet, whichever is greater		Quantity extra	Distributor discounts
Under	150	200%	12.5%
150 to "	300	125%	10. %
300 to "	600	85%	10. %
600 to "	1,250	55%	10. %
1,250 to "	2,500	27.5%	10. %
2,500 to "	5,000	12.5%	7.5%
5,000 to "	10,000	7.5%	6. %
10,000 to "	20,000	5.%	5. %

To show how the cost is calculated, we may assume that our product is 1.5″ O.D. x .110 mechanical tubing, random lengths, purchased in the 1,250 to under 2,500 pound order-quantity bracket. (Calculations based on pounds, since pounds greater than feet)

$14.305 — price base per 100 pounds
x   1.61   (61% product extra)
——————————
$23.03 = product base per 100 pounds

     plus   27.5% quantity extra (1,250 to under 2,500 bracket)
    minus   5.0% random length deduction
Net plus $\overline{22.5\%}$ = 1.225 x $23.03 per 100 lbs. = $28.21 net at the
                    producing mill.

Minus 10% distributor discount, equals .90 x $28.21 = $25.39 before
freight is added to get the delivered price per 100 pounds. With a
freight cost of $1.50 per 100 pounds the delivered price would be
$26.89 per 100 pounds.

As the example illustrates, the regular "quantity extra" is a
summation extra, which is added together with a number of other
"extras" or "deductions." For example, a "specially smooth O.D."
carries a 40% extra, a given chemical requirement might add 15%
extra, random length carries a 5% deduction, etc. These extras or
deductions are summed along with the quantity extra, and the net
percentage, plus or minus, is applied to increase or decrease the
product base, as shown in the example. The distributor *discounts
apply* to the final calculated price before freight. Thus, the distributor
discounts are applied to a different base than the regular quantity extra
percentage. In addition, the distributor discounts *decrease* with increased order-quantity sizes, thus tending to counteract the attractive-
ness of the regular quantity extra savings from moving into higher
order-quantity brackets.

Continuing with our example, assume that we were to purchase
the 1.5″ O.D. x .110 mechanical tubing in the next higher order-quantity bracket. The cost calculation would be:

            $23.03 = product base per 100 pounds
   plus   12.5% quantity extra (2,500 to under 5,000 bracket)
  minus   5.0% random length deduction
 Net plus $\overline{7.5\%}$ = 1.075 x $23.03 = $24.76 per 100 pounds at
                  the producing mill.

Minus 7.5% distributor discount, equals .925 x $24.76, or $22.90 per
100 pounds before freight. With freight of $1.50 per 100 pounds, the
delivered price would be $24.40.

Thus, by buying in a 2,500 pound quantity we have a $2.49 saving
per 100 pounds (i.e., $26.89 − $24.40). Now that we have this unit
saving we are in a position to determine what the DPY should be
before we would want to buy in 2,500 pound quantities. Assume that
our CPO = $4.00, and our COP = 12%.

When purchased in 1250 quantity:
    Ordering cost = \$4./12.5 = \$ .32 per 100 pounds
    Material cost = \$26.89 per 100 pounds
    Annual holding cost = 12.5/2 x \$26.89 x .12 = \$20.17
When purchased in 2500 quantity:
    Ordering cost = \$./25. = \$ .16 per 100 pounds
    Material cost = \$22.90 per 100 pounds
    Annual holding cost = 25./2 x \$22.90 x .12 = \$34.35

We are now in a position to calculate the "point of indifference" between buying in 1250 or 2500 pound quantities. Our formula:

$$\text{DPY} = \frac{\text{Increased annual holding costs}}{\text{Savings per unit when buying in 2500 pound quantity}}$$

$$= \frac{\$34.35 - \$20.17}{(\$.32 - \$.16) + (\$26.89 - \$22.90)} = \frac{\$14.18}{\$2.65}$$

$$= 5.35 \text{ hundred pounds}$$

At a DPY of 5.35 hundred pounds our TACIM will be the same whether we purchase in the 1250 or 2500 pound order-quantity bracket. If DPY is less than 5.35 hundred pounds the material should be purchased in 12.50 hundred quantities; if greater than 5.35 hundred pounds the material should be purchased in *at least* 25 hundred-pound quantities. We can only say "*at least* 25 hundred pound quantities" since we must still consider the possibility that we should be buying in, say, the next larger order-quantity bracket, i.e., in the 50 hundred pound order-quantity bracket. Calculation of the points of indifference between successively higher order-quantity brackets will indicate the rate of demand at which it would be desirable to purchase in ever larger quantities. In other words, the "next higher" price-break order quantity becomes progressively more attractive as the monthly demand increases, as was first pointed out in Chapter 6, and shown graphically in Figure 6-1.

difficulty in preparing order-quantity tables

Having just pointed out how DPY "points of indifference" may be calculated when percentage quantity extras apply, one may ask: How does this differ significantly from the preparation of ordering tables covering hot-rolled bars, et al., as explained earlier? The problem is that the *effective* percentage quantity extra differs with each different set of "summation" extras. For example, assume that all factors were the same as in our previous example of the 1.5" x .110 mechanical tubing, *except* that we wanted a "specially smooth O.D." at 40% extra, and a chemical requirement that called for a 15% extra. While our product base would remain the same, i.e., $23.03 per 100 pounds, the final cost will be substantially higher because of the additional extras. For example:

Plus	$23.03	= product base
Plus	27.5%	quantity extra (1250 lb. quantity bracket)
Plus	40.0%	specially smooth O.D.
Minus	15. %	chemical extra
	5. %	random length
Net plus	77.5%	= 1.775 x $23.03 = $40.88

Minus 10% distributor discount, equals .90 x $40.88 = $36.79. With freight included, the delivered price would be $38.29 per 100 pounds.

A similar calculation covering the 2500 pound order quantity results in a cost of $36.11 per 100 pounds. The resulting DPY point of indifference between ordering 1250 and 2500 pound quantities now becomes 10.88 hundred pounds—a sharp increase over the 5.35 hundred pounds point of indifference previously calculated.

In our former example the price per 100 pound differential between 1250 and 2500 quantities was $2.49 (i.e., $26.89 − $24.40) Now, because of the manner in which the quantity extra and distributor discounts work out, the differential is only $2.18 (i.e., $38.29 − $36.11) per hundred pounds. The sharp rise in the point of indifference is thus a result of two factors. First, the direct material cost saving is less, and secondly, because of the increased AHC because of the more expensive material.

If one wanted absolute precision therefore, it would be necessary to prepare a great number of ordering tables to guide the selection of the optimum order quantity. As a practical matter, however, is it really necessary to have absolute precision? For example, in the example previously presented, the "point of indifference" between 1250 and 2500 units increased from 5.35 to 10.88 hundred pounds as the net "extras plus deductions" (not including the quantity extra") increased from a 5% deduction to a 50% extra. With this particular knowledge we might want to interpolate the point of indifference when the net "extras plus deductions" were, say, 22.5% (i.e., one-half the distance between −5% and +50%). One might interpolate the point of indifference as being 8.1 hundred pounds (i.e., the middle point between 5.35 and 10.88). The actual calculation of such a point shows it to be 8.5 hundred pounds, within a reasonable margin of the 8.1 interpolated point of indifference.

summary

The goal of this chapter has been to demonstrate a method whereby ordering tables may be prepared to efficiently determine the optimum order quantity in which items should be replenished. Three types of tables may be required.

1. *For hot-rolled bars, et al., where "all units" discounts apply, and where minimum order quantity is higher than the "Q" which would result from the economic order quantity formula, the tables are relatively easily developed.*
2. *For items such as structural shapes, for example, where base cost applies for minimum order quantities, it was shown how the EOQ formula could either be used directly or could be adapted to simplify the determination of that point, in DPY, where one might want to order in a predetermined order size.*
3. *For those metal items where percentage quantity extras apply, and where the calculations are somewhat more complex, a number of tables may be required, along with interpolation. Here, more so than with the other classes of metal items, a computer would be of great help in making calculations.*

In all cases, the calculations are dependent upon the use of input data in the form of estimated costs of possession and order costs. The estimation of these costs will be the topic of Chapter 8.

8 data input: estimating costs

IF ONE WERE TO POINT OUT the two broad areas of difficulty, or potential stumbling blocks, in the understanding and application of inventory theory and control, these would be: 1) the understanding of the *manner* in which inventory theory and models may be used to determine optimal ordering rules and inventory policy, and 2) the estimation of the costs necessary in the use of the various models. The first of these two areas has been dealt with in the preceding chapters, which started out with a simple inventory problem under certainty, and gradually introduced the problems of uncertainties, quantity extras, forecasting demand, the steel inventory system, and the manner in which optimum order quantities and reorder points could be determined. The present chapter deals with the estimation of the costs needed to make use of the inventory theory and models thus far presented. More specifically, this chapter deals with the estimation of the cost of possession (COP), ordering costs (CPO), and stockout costs (SC). Each of these costs will be taken up in some detail, but before plunging into this task it seems worthwhile to consider briefly the general nature of the costs with which we will be dealing.

difficulties in estimation of costs

First of all, none of these costs appear, as such, in regular accounting records. Secondly, each firm must estimate its own costs based upon the unique set of cost factors and economic relationships pertinent to its own operation. Thus it is hazardous to "borrow" someone else's figures and expect them to have fully valid relevance to your own system. Third, in the estimation of these costs it is necessary to make use of such concepts as opportunity (alternate) costs, fixed-variable costs, etc; and in many cases these are cost concepts which are unfamiliar.

A further difficulty relates to the *source* of the data used in making such cost estimates. Almost inevitably this source is at least partially historical accounting data, whereas *future* costs are what we want to minimize. Hence, it is appropriate to talk about *estimated future costs,*

155

which may be developed through the use of historical accounting data, executive judgment, and other sources.

A final difficulty relates to the *precision* of the required estimates. The greater the precision of the estimates the greater is the cost of their development. More will be said about this later.

The preceding paragraphs may well convince one that the task of estimating costs is really too formidable to be tackled, and that more questions will be raised than can be answered. To counter this feeling it seems wise to make some (hopefully) optimistic comments concerning the task of estimating the type of costs needed. First, of course, it is not really possible to avoid the task of estimating costs. No matter what means are used in arriving at inventory decisions, there are underlying explicit *or* implicit estimates of costs involved in such decisions. Secondly, as will be pointed out in more detail later, total costs are relatively insensitive to moderate errors in estimating input costs. For example, if through error a COP of .16 is used, when the "true" COP should be .18 or .19, the total cost will vary by a considerably smaller magnitude than the magnitude of the error in estimating the COP.

With no further preliminaries it seems wise to look more closely at the makeup of some of the elements of the cost of possession, ordering cost, and stockout cost. In the analysis of what goes into each of these costs it will be appropriate to indicate some of the thinking or methodology underlying its determination.

COST OF POSSESSION

The cost of possession, or inventory holding cost, may be best understood by considering the cost elements generally included in it. The following list, while not exhaustive, includes most of the normally included elements.

> Cost of invested capital
> Insurance
> Taxes
> Storage facilities and space charges
> Accounting (clerical, inventory taking, etc.)
> Deterioration and spoilage
> Obsolescence

It is immediately obvious that these individual costs are not readily available from traditional accounting records and reports. None the less, through a rearrangement of existing accounting data many of the costs may be reasonably closely estimated. Even should there be difficulty in arriving at what are believed to be reliable estimates, it is wise to bear in mind that these are the types of cost information which are of great value for decision-making purposes in areas other than inventory management. Hence, there is much to suggest the wisdom of whatever study is required to produce appropriate figures.

cost of invested capital

This particular cost is frequently the largest of the elements making up the total cost-of-possession figure. The determination of this cost factor has been a troublesome one, since to adequately calculate the "cost" of capital it is necessary to make use of the "opportunity" or "alternative" cost concept. In addition, as will be pointed out, there are several pitfalls to be avoided in determining this important element in the total cost-of-possession figure.

At the outset it may be worthwhile to point out that historically there has been more of an emphasis on getting a return on invested capital, and the "cost of capital" concept has been (perhaps) slighted. One of the side benefits of inventory theory applications has been that it has brought into focus the important concept of "cost of capital," and particularly the opportunity cost concept. Perhaps a meaningful way to introduce this concept is to make use of an example.

Assume that in a given firm it is possible to shrink the inventory by $10,000. This could be done by reducing safety (buffer) stocks and/or by ordering in smaller order quantities. What might be done with this $10,000? Or, to put the question differently: What are the "opportunities" for the investment of this $10,000? If it were used to reduce a 5% interest bank loan, then we would say that the opportunity cost of the $10,000 was 5%. Suppose, however, that we could invest this money in a piece of processing equipment where the return would be 20%? In this case the opportunity cost would be 20%. Suppose that the $10,000 could be used to retire some stock. If the stockholders could invest this money where the return was 10%, for example, then one would have to say (at least from the stockholders' viewpoint) that the money had an opportunity cost of 10%. At the minimum, of course, this $10,000 could be invested in government bonds for a guaranteed return of from 3% to 4%.

The key question is this: What is the cost of the $10,000 *if it remains in inventory?* The opportunity cost doctrine says that the cost is the highest of the returns available from alternative uses. In the illustration used this would be 20%, the return we might get if we invested in the processing equipment. Thus, *if* we keep the $10,000 in inventory we must forego a return of 20% which we can get if we invest the money in the processing equipment.

inventory as an earning asset

Operating experience in the metal industry clearly indicates that inventories may be relatively larger or smaller, depending upon the operating philosophy and practices of the management. Hence, it is reasonable to suggest that this experience indicates that total inventory investment is subject to alternative operating levels, and that the level chosen is (or *should* be) *dependent* upon the return on investment which a given operating doctrine provides. For example, in the preceding illustration, assume that the $10,000 would provide a 25% return on investment *when invested in inventory*. Then it is quite clear that this is where the money should be. However, suppose that the extra (or marginal) investment in the inventory, which usually is the investment to support high safety stocks or the extra investment when buying in larger order quantities, is returning only a 10% return. In this later case, clearly, it would be more profitable to strip this money from inventory and invest it in the processing equipment where the return would be 20%.

knowledge of investment opportunities

The preceding discussion assumes the existence of knowledge of alternative investment opportunities. This in itself may not be a realistic assumption. Quite commonly there is no available information concerning the opportunities for alternative investments. An earlier reference was made to one of the side benefits of the application of inventory theory. In order to arrive at the true "cost" of money tied up in inventory, it is necessary to evaluate the alternative investment opportunities. This endeavor in itself may provide some highly beneficial information for decision-making purposes, and if an endeavor to apply inventory theory adds impetus to the development of alternative investment opportunities, then this in itself is an important side benefit from giving attention to inventory theory implementation.

"new capital" pitfall

An implicit assumption, particularly for the short run, is that there is a limited amount of capital, and that it is management's task

be helpful to keep several thoughts in mind when developing these estimates. First, these costs *do* exist: the problem is that of producing a reasonable estimate of the magnitude of the costs which should apply to various classes of metal items. Second, these particular costs, stated in terms of a percent of dollar cost of inventory per year, are added with a number of other elements to arrive at the total cost of possession. While the estimates for any one of the elements may be over or under the "true" cost, it may be anticipated that these plus and minus figures will "wash out" when the elements are summed.

ordering costs

The term "ordering cost" is somewhat of a misnomer, since this cost includes many factors other than the actual ordering of the material. For example, while the purchasing department will typically fill out the purchase order, it will be necessary for the order to be typed, for copies of the order to be filed or acted upon in various departments, perhaps to have expenses for expediting, receiving and inspection of materials, the auditing and payment of the bills for the material, etc.

A commonly employed means of estimating this ordering cost is as follows: Assume a 25% *increase* in the number of orders submitted. The reason for this assumption is to develop the *marginal* or variable costs associated with this increase in the number of orders. Thus, assume that a given operating doctrine or policy has resulted in 200 orders per month. What would be the *change* in costs were the ordering rate to increase to 250 per month? Perhaps one-fourth the time of a typist would be required in the purchasing department, an extra 30 hours of direct labor in the receiving department, etc. In other words, certain costs would increase because of the increase in orders from 200 to 250 per month.

While many costs would increase as a result of the increased number of orders, others would *not* increase at all. Certain expenses such as heat and light would not change. Furthermore, the salaries of supervisory personnel would not likely change. These costs are in the nature of fixed or semi-fixed costs, and would not vary with the change in the rate at which purchase orders are submitted.

When all of the increased costs have been estimated it is an easy task to divide the increased costs by the increased number of orders. In the example being used, assume that the increased costs for paperwork, receiving, extra materials handling, accounts payable, etc., were estimated at $350 for the additional 50 orders. The variable costs per order would then be seven dollars, and this is the figure which would be used in the various inventory models previously presented.

direct observation of ordering procedure

Another means of estimating the ordering cost is to make a direct observation of what's involved in the procedure. This study would begin with the first step in the ordering procedure—more than likely in the purchasing department when a purchase order is filled out. The time of a buyer to fill out the purchase order, perhaps with multiple items per order, would be recorded. The flow of the paperwork would be noted, including the time required by those who file, process, or take action on such purchasing and/or accounts payable procedures. In addition, direct observation in the receiving-warehouse operation would provide a basis for estimating the time per order for this portion of the operation. The advantage of this direct observation method is that potential improvements in procedures may be noted at the same time that information is obtained for estimating the ordering cost. In addition, at each step of the direct observation it will be necessary to ask: What would be the effect of an increase in the *rate* at which orders are being submitted? It is quite clear that those parts of the operation where an *increase* in this rate can be handled at no apparent increase in cost are in the nature of *fixed* costs. Thus, for example, were it judged not to be necessary to hire any extra typists when the rate of purchase orders is increased by 25%, it is apparent that our typists are not being currently utilized to their full capacity.

potential for underestimating cost

There is a pitfall to be avoided in estimating the ordering cost. In any given organization, at any given time, certain practices exist. To carry out these practices there are a number of personnel, following certain procedures in relation to all the activities necessary for the replenishment of stock. Whatever number of people there are may be considered as "fixed" in nature, at least in the short run. Thus, within a reasonable range of increased or decreased business activity the personnel would remain fixed in number. In what could be suggested as an example of Parkinson's Law these personnel will increase or decrease their work pace to meet the needs of the firm at any given time. Now, along comes an analyst who is attempting to determine the "ordering" cost. Someone else in the firm may very well suggest to the analyst: "It's *not* going to cost us anything to order more frequently. A greater number of orders will just take up the slack." Perhaps this is true, *in the short run* and within reasonable ranges of activity. Aside from the short run, however, increased business activity and growth will sooner or later bring about the need for another typist, another man in the receiving department, etc., and another cycle will have begun. Perhaps what is being suggested is this: "In the long run there is no such thing as a *fixed* cost." To the extent that this is true it is hazardous to deal with cost estimating as though always moving from one short-run period to another, since this can produce a severe under-estimation of costs.

stockout costs

The term "stockout cost" is a rather broad one, and unless it is more fully defined it may not be known just what a person means when using the term. Part of this confusion may be avoided by distinguishing between a "stockout" which results in a lost sale, and the "backordering" case, in which the customer is willing to wait a reasonable time for delivery (of either all of the amount ordered, or for the balance to follow a partial delivery).

While all inventory managers sooner or later are involved in talking about stockout costs, it is often difficult to get estimates of such costs. Various studies and research bear out this point. The estimation of stockout costs is particularly difficult when dealing with a differentiated product. For example, if the Florsheim shoe store is out of your shoe size you may walk down the street to the Nunn-Bush shoe store where they do have your size, and in the process may discover that you like Nunn-Bush as well as or better than the Florsheim brand. In such a case the Florsheim dealer has lost not only the gross profit from this one sale, but the gross profit from all the other shoes you would have purchased over the years. Here the "loss of good will" is of considerable consequence, and is particularly difficult to estimate.

While the preceding illustration is appropriate for a differentiated product such as shoes, it is not so meaningful for *non-differentiated* products. With non-differentiated products, which properly describes many metal items, a stockout is not nearly so likely to result in the loss of good will, simply because delivery can still be made through picking up the metal items at a secondary source of supply. Thus, in a wide segment of the metals industry the difficult problem of "loss of good will" is avoided.

survey of stockout penalties

A Metals Service Center research study, conducted in 1963-64, included a question about stockout penalties. Of the 232 replies to an inventory management questionnaire, fifty-five companies answered that they had calculated (or estimated) the financial loss or penalty resulting from being "out-of-stock" of an item normally carried in stock. The questionnaire suggested three categories of penalties, or costs, and included additional space for "other" costs which respondents could fill in. Following are the results:

Number	Penalty included:
19	Gross profit only
15	Expense required to get material from competitors
20	Both gross profit loss plus expense required to get material from competitors

In addition, one respondent answered that added delivery trips were included in the penalty, and another added "customer confidence in delivery source." It is of interest that out of the fifty-five replies there was only one reply which could be considered in the nature of a "good-will" loss. The predominate reason for this, it is believed, is because of the *service* commitment on the part of a wide segment of the metals industry, which results in the supply of the demanded item from a secondary source—thus avoiding the loss of good will.

loss of gross profit margin

Perhaps it is best at the outset to suggest that no one can *precisely* calculate what a given stockout will cost. This is simply because there are a number of cost and profit relationships which will determine a specific stockout cost. For example, when a stockout occurs is the material picked up from a competitor? If so, is just enough material picked up to fill the order, or is an extra amount picked up to fill whatever additional demand may occur before the stock item is replenished? At what price is the material picked up from the competitor in relation to the selling price of the material to the customer? Perhaps the customer is purchasing a number of items for which he will be getting a quantity deduction, whereas the one item picked up to fill his order carries no such quantity deduction. What about the cost of sending a truck to pick up the material? These and other questions merely illustrate the complexity which may result in attempting to determine *precisely* what a stockout will cost. Fortunately, a reasonable approximation to the stockout cost may be arrived at by evaluating the gross profit margins applying to given classes of products.

As used here, the gross margin is the difference between net sales and cost of goods sold. Such data is usually available from accounting and/or sales analysis reports. Assume, for example, that for a given class of metal items the gross margin is 25% *over cost*. This would be the case, for example, if material cost $10.00 per hundred pounds and was being sold for $12.50 per hundred pounds. This margin of $2.50 per hundred pounds must cover selling, delivery, and other operating expenses. Subtracting these operating expenses from gross margin results in the net margin, which in turn may have to cover other types of expense before the remaining balance may be viewed as net profit. If, then, we received an order for 100 pounds of this material, and found it necessary to pick up the material from a competitor, it is reasonable to assume that we have lost a minimum of $2.50 on the order. The *assumption* underlying this hypothesis is that our *operating expenses are going to be the same as if we had filled the order from our own inventory*. A further assumption is that the 100 pounds of material will cost us $12.50, the same amount we will receive from our customer. *If* we could have supplied the 100 pounds from our own stock we would have had the $2.50 to apply toward covering our operating expenses. By being forced to pick up the material we have $2.50 less to apply to our operating expenses, and in addition our operating expenses are no less because we picked up 100 pounds of material from our competitor.

The preceding analysis could be restated many different ways, depending upon what assumptions one might want to make. On the basis of certain assumptions the stockout cost would be *less* than the $2.50 gross margin, while other assumptions would result in a loss *greater* than the gross margin. What is suggested is that the gross margin is a reasonable beginning point for whatever additional adjustments it is felt would produce a closer estimate. These additional refinements must be arrived at by each individual firm. For example, one firm may find it necessary to include an additional cost because of the expense of sending trucks to pick up material from competitors. Yet another firm might not include this cost because their own trucks are on such a schedule that in the normal course of events they would be in areas where pickups may be required.

stockout cost in percentage terms

The practical advantage from using the gross margin percentage (adjusted up or down as further refinements are judged necessary) is that a *percentage* stockout is thus developed. This is highly useful in calculating the optimum probability of filling all demand during lead time. By having both the cost of possession (COP) and the stockout cost (SC) in percentage terms, it is possible to calculate this optimum probability easily. One point of some importance is to have each percentage calculated on the same base. For example, the cost of possession is almost always viewed as the cost, in decimal fraction terms, of keeping a dollar tied up in inventory for a year. Thus, a COP of 25% means that it costs .25 of a dollar to keep a dollar tied up in inventory for a year. Now, if our stockout cost is also stated in percentage terms, and applies to the same dollar base as the COP does, we may use this to advantage in either a computerized program or in developing tables of various sorts. For example, if the SC turned out to be 25% this would mean that our stockout cost was .25 of the cost of goods (CPU) as carried on the inventory records.

total cost sensitivity to estimating errors

Difficulties in estimating input costs have been one of the reasons why inventory theory and control practices are not in more widespread use. These difficulties are readily apparent from the foregoing discussion of the estimation of the cost of possession, ordering costs, and stockout costs. None of these costs may be estimated with absolute precision. Fortunately, such precision is not necessary to make effective use of inventory models. This is because the total cost is *relatively* insensitive to errors in estimating input costs.

To illustrate this insensitivity let us make use of the inventory model under certainty, with no quantity discounts.

Optimum Q is:

$$Q = \sqrt{\frac{2 \times DPY \times CPO}{CPU \times COP}}$$

Total variable costs are:

$$TAC = (Q/2 \times CPU \times COP) + (DPY/Q \times CPO)$$

Let us now consider the effect on "Q" and TAC when there are errors in estimating the "true" cost of CPO and COP. We may rewrite the formula for Q as follows:

$$Q = \sqrt{\frac{2 \times DPY}{CPU}} \times \sqrt{\frac{CPO}{COP}}$$

This enables us to check directly the change in the order quantity in relation to the "correctness" of the square root of CPO/COP. Only four cases will be used, since these effectively bracket the correct (i.e., 100%) relationship between CPO/COP.

Assume CPO/COP is the following percentage of "true" cost	Q will be this percentage of the optimum Q	Additional TAC will be:
50%	71%	6%
100%	100%	0%
150%	122%	2%
200%	141%	6%

When CPO/COP is 50% this could be because: COP was correct, but CPO was only 50% of true; COP was 125% of true, while CPO was only 62% of true, etc. In each case the resulting fraction is .5, of which the square root is .71, thus resulting in a Q which is 71% of the optimum. Several important relationships are shown. First, the errors in estimating CPO and COP are minimized because Q is the result of the square root of CPO/COP. Secondly, the additional TAC is only a fraction of the error in determining the optimum Q. Thus, when Q is only 71% of optimum, the annual holding cost (Q/2 x CPU x COP) will be lower than they would be had Q been at the optimum level, and this saving will tend to compensate for the increase in annual ordering costs (DPY/Q x CPO) brought about by the less-than-optimum Q. A third point that should be made is that *both* CPO and COP may be in error, and yet the optimum Q could still be obtained. This would be the result, for example, when each estimate was 25% too high, in which case the fraction CPO/COP would still be 100%.

The foregoing illustration suggests that we are dealing with a relatively flat total cost curve, particularly around the optimum point. When this is the case, as is frequently true, total costs will not vary substantially with reasonable variances from the "true" cost for ordering and cost of possession.

stockout cost sensitivity

An analysis similar to the above may be made for the sensitivity to errors in the estimation of stockout costs. Assume that a stockout cost has been *overestimated*. What is the net result of such an error? First of all, the calculated "probability of filling all demand during lead time" will be higher than it should be. The net result will be that there will be higher safety stocks than there would have been had the "true" stockout cost been used in the calculation. Here again, however, there is a compensating saving, since the higher safety stocks mean that we will be filling a higher percentage of demand during lead time, and thus there will be a lower "understock" cost. Here again we are dealing with a total cost curve, and one which is frequently relatively "flat" within a reasonable distance either side of the optimum (minimum cost) point on the curve.

summary

This chapter began by pointing out that the estimation of input data was no easy task, and in fact that difficulties in this regard have prevented a more widespread application of inventory theory and control systems. Many of the "conceptual" difficulties involved in the estimation of the cost of possession, ordering costs, and stockout costs have been dealt with. Through the utilization of reformulated historical accounting data, executive judgment, and other sources it is believed that adequate estimates may be arrived at, *without* unreaosnable cost in time and effort. The precision of the estimates must be considered in relationship to the total cost sensitivity of the inventory models used. As was shown, total costs are typically not sensitive to reasonable variation from the "true" values of the cost of possession, ordering cost, and stockout cost.

9 the complete algorithm and some comments on computerized inventory systems

IN THIS CHAPTER WE WILL SUMMARIZE the steps of the algorithm. Our summary will describe the procedure which should be employed to calculate:

Q, the optimum order quantity;
and   R, the optimum reorder point

The algorithm is summarized in the form of a flow diagram in Figure 9-1. The sample procedure portrayed in Figure 9-1 is based on the assumption that quantity extras are quoted, that there is a *minimum* order quantity, that forecasts have already been made of DDLT (demand during lead time) and V (the variance of the demand during lead time forecast), and that therefore the following pertinent data are given:

DDLT = the mean of the demand during lead time forecast, in hundred lbs.

V   = the variance of the demand during lead time forecast, in hundred lbs.

DPY = the demand forecast for one year, in hundred lbs.

COP = cost of possession, in percent of investment per year

CPO = the cost of processing a purchase order

SC   = the stockout cost in dollars/hundred lbs. short

CPU = the delivered cost per hundred lbs. associated with the order quantity under consideration

The algorithm of Figure 9-1 calls for the employment of Tables 1, 2 and 3 of Appendix B and the following models, discussed in previous chapters:
Model 3-3:

171

$$Q = \sqrt{\frac{2 \times DPY(CPO + E(DDLT > R) \times SC)}{COP \times CPU}}$$

Model 3-4:

$$P(DDLT > R) = \frac{CPU \times COP \times Q}{DPY \times SC + CPU \times COP \times Q}$$

Model 7-1:

$$TACIM_Q = [Q/2 \times CPU_Q \times COP] + [DPY/Q \times CPO] + [DPY \times CPU_Q]$$

. . . in which Q takes on, successively, the order quantity associated with the minimum order quantity and the order quantities associated with the various price breaks.

some comments on exhaustiveness in models and the cost of information

The flow diagram of Figure 9-1 calls into play models 3-3, 3-4 and 7-1. The algorithm of Figure 9-1 is itself a model, however. All models are abstractions, and none fully represents the system it is designed to simulate. No model is more valid than the assumptions which underlie it.

If the cost of information were negligible we would want to employ extremely exhaustive models. In fact, if the cost of information were zero we would literally operate the system under forecast conditions, trying all possible combinations of policies, to arrive at the optimum policy.

However, the cost of information is not zero. Furthermore, there is an increasing marginal cost associated with information: the more information we seek the more costly "equal additional increments" of information become. As progress is made in the science of management decision and as the cost of computation decreases, we can afford more information and therefore we insist on progressively more exhaustive models.

A model like that portrayed in Figure 9-1 would have been unlikely 20 years ago. But with improved understanding of the metal inventory system and with decreased computation cost it is today thoroughly practicable.

As the cost of computation continues to decrease we will want to make our model more exhaustive yet. For example, we will want to expand Tables 2 and 3 in Appendix B. In the design of the tables we limited our choice in order to keep the tables small. Our objective was to keep these tables within the memory capacity of small commercial computers so that memory space would not preclude introduction of a computerized system for small metal service centers.

By so limiting ourselves, however, we pay a price in accuracy, and as further strides are made in hardware design we will want to make

FIGURE   9-1

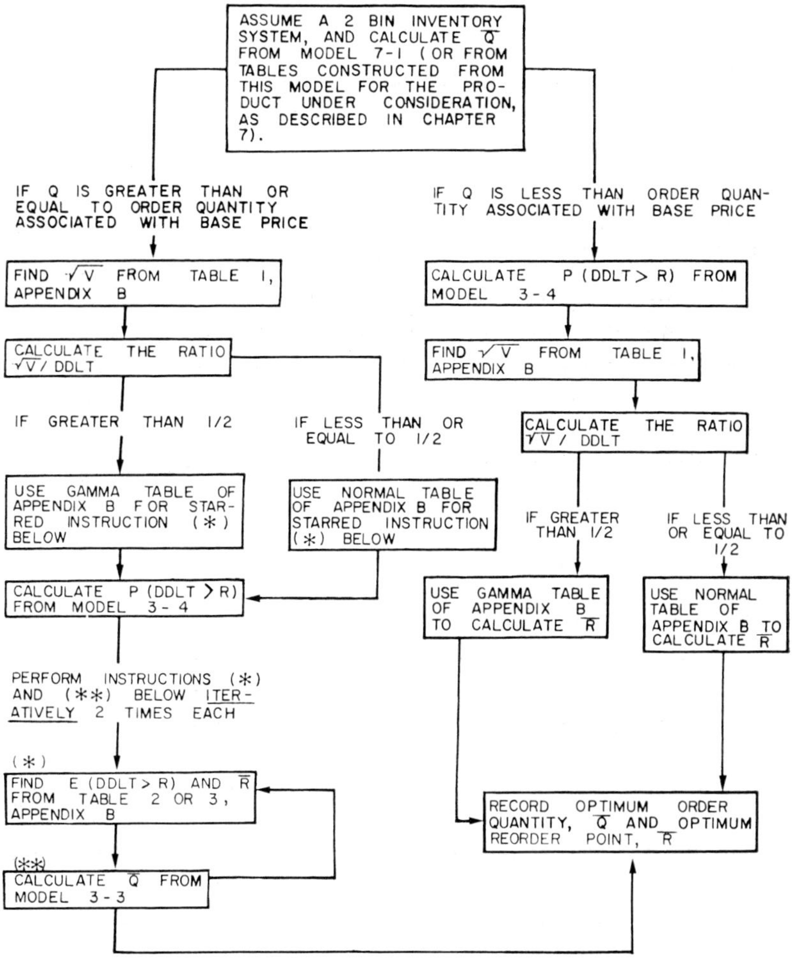

this and other alterations in our model so that it becomes more exhaustive.

In retrospect it may appear that the model of Figure 9-1 is already burdensome and badly suited to a non-computerized system. In this regard it should be pointed out that for many metal service centers, buying in quantities less than that required for enjoying the base price is common for most products. Under these circumstances only the right half of Figure 9-1 is required. In a hand-operated system, policy could be reviewed for a particular product using a desk calculator in only a few minutes. The operation can be further simplified by the use of tables (called for in the first step of Figure 9-1) developed by a simple computer program, and further by the use of nomographs which can be developed as a substitute for the gamma tables of Appendix B.

For centers desiring to rent computing time from Data Service Centers, in order to make periodic policy review, any reasonably competent programmer employee at one of these centers can compose a program suitable for the appropriate data processing system from the algorithm of Figure 9-1.

As suggested previously all models fall short of fully representing the system they are designed to simulate. For this reason the applicability of any model is restricted and the knowledgeable manager will know when to "preempt control" from a routinized policy determination system when conditions warrant. The chapters preceding the presentation of the algorithm of Figure 9-1 have been designed to convey the understanding required for optimum use of the models which this volume discusses.

appendix A

demand during lead time distribution via monte carlo simulation

The two discrete distributions discussed in Chapter 3—the daily demand distribution and the lead time distribution—could be combined to yield a single probability distribution for demand during lead time by Monte Carlo simulation.

One way to do this would involve sampling colored balls from two jars. We could place together in a jar 4 white balls, 3 blue balls, 2 yellow balls, and 1 green ball. Then, if we drew a ball at random, recorded its color, replaced it and drew another, recorded its color, replaced it, etc., stirring the balls each time, we would expect that if we continued this sampling process long enough 40 percent of the time we would find ourselves drawing white balls, 30 percent of the time blue balls, 20 percent of the time yellow balls, and 10 percent of the time green balls. To simulate the wholesaler's expected daily demand pattern, we simply consider the "drawing of a ball" to be the "simulation of a day's operation," equating

> White balls as demand for 0 units;
> Blue balls as demand for 1 unit;
> Yellow balls as demand for 2 units;
> Green balls as demand for 3 units.

If a white ball is drawn, we reason that on that simulated "day of operations" 0 units of Item A were demanded; if a blue ball is drawn 1 unit was demanded; if a yellow ball is drawn 2 units were demanded; and if a green ball is drawn 3 units were demanded. Since we have loaded the jar with 4 white balls, 3 blue balls, 2 yellow balls, and 1 green ball, over the long run 0 units will be demanded 40 percent of the days; 1 unit will be demanded 30 percent of the days; 2 units will be demanded 20 percent of the days, and 3 units will be demanded 10

175

percent of the days. Thus our sampling process will perfectly simulate the wholesaler's expected daily demand pattern.

In the same way we could simulate the wholesaler's expected lead time pattern. In a separate jar 25 white balls might be deposited to represent a lead time of 1 day; 50 blue balls for a lead time of 2 days; and 25 yellow balls for a lead time of 3 days.

simulating the wholesaler's demand during lead time

Now, to simulate demand during lead time, we would proceed as follows:

1. Draw a ball from jar two (representing lead time):
   a) If a white ball was drawn, we reason that in our first "simulated experience" lead time was one day. Therefore we draw one ball from jar one (representing daily demand). If we draw a white ball from jar one, we record "demand zero." If we draw a blue ball, we record "demand 1"; if a yellow ball, "demand 2," etc.
   b) If a blue ball was drawn, we reason that in our first "simulated experience" lead time was two days, so we draw one ball from jar one, record our experience, replace the ball and draw another ball, record our experience, and add up the resulting "demands" for the two days in order to determine total demand during the two days of lead time.
   c) If a yellow ball was drawn, we proceed as above, but we draw from jar one three times.
2. Draw a second ball from jar two to simulate a second lead time experience, and proceed as in a), b), and c) above.
3. Draw a third ball from jar two to simulate a third lead time experience, and proceed as in a), b), and c) above, etc.

If we continued this simulation process over a large number of trials we would expect to find that a demand during lead time (DDLT) of 9 units would occur 0.03 percent of the time—and that a DDLT of 8 units would occur 0.15 percent of the time—since we have already developed these probabilities analytically.

Where a great number of combinations of demands per day and lead time duration are possible an analytical solution becomes impracticable and Monte Carlo simulation is very useful.

In actual practice, however, we do not use colored balls but rather a random number list. In a list of two-digit random numbers each number is as likely to occur next (reading the list from the top down, for example) as any other two-digit number; and we can cause the "reading of a number" to be the equivalent of "drawing a ball" by the following scheme:

Let number 00	through number 39	represent a demand for 0 units
" 40	69	1 unit
" 70	89	2 units
" 90	99	3 units

And

Let number 00	through number 24	represent a lead time of 1 day
" 25	74	2 days
" 75	99	3 days

We now "read a number" from our two-digit random number list to determine the number of days in our simulated lead time; and, depending on the outcome, read 1, 2, or 3 numbers to determine total demand during lead time for that simulated lead time experience.

This process of reading a number and recording its interpretation in terms of the system being simulated would be cumbersome if we were obliged to do it in the fashion described above. However, by use of the computer, Monte Carlo simulation can be made easily manageable.

In most inventory systems it is possible to avoid Monte Carlo simulation altogether by using continuous rather than discrete probability distributions, as shown in Chapter 5.

appendix B
probability tables for calculating the optimum reorder point and the expected stockout during lead time associated with it

DATA REQUIRED

Q = the order quantity, in hundred lbs.

$DDLT$ = the mean of the demand during lead time forecast, in hundred lbs.

V = the variance of the demand during lead time forecast, in hundred lbs.

CPU = the delivered cost per hundred lbs. associated with the order quantity, Q

COP = the cost of possession, in percent of investment, per year

DPY = the demand forecast for one year, in hundred lbs.

SC = the cost of running short 100 hundred lbs.

PROCEDURE

DETERMINE $\sqrt{V}$ FROM THE SQUARE ROOT TABLE (Table 1). IF $\sqrt{V}$/DDLT IS LESS THAN ½ USE THE NORMAL TABLE (Table 2). OTHERWISE USE THE GAMMA TABLE (Table 3).

TO USE THE NORMAL TABLE (Table 2):

Step 1: Calculate the optimum probability of a stockout during time, $P(DDLT > R)$:

$$(P(DDLT > R) = \frac{CPU \times COP \times Q}{DPY \times SC + CPU \times COP \times Q}$$

Step 2: Refer to the NORMAL table (Table 2). Opposite that value for $P(DDLT > R)$ which is closest* to the value for $P(DDLT > R)$ calculated in Step 1 above, read factors F1 and F2

TO CALCULATE THE EXPECTED STOCKOUT DURING LEAD TIME, $E(DDLT > R)$:
$$E(DDLT > R) = F2 \times \sqrt{V}$$
TO CALCULATE THE OPTIMUM REORDER POINT, R:
$$R = DDLT + F1 \times \sqrt{V}$$

TO USE THE GAMMA TABLE (Table 3):

Step 1: Calculate the optimum probability of a stockout during lead time, $P(DDLT > R)$:

$$P(DDLT > R) = \frac{CPU \times COP \times Q}{DPY \times SC + CPU \times COP \times Q}$$

Step 2: Calculate L: $L = DDLT/V$

Step 3: Calculate R1: $R1 = DDLT \times L$

Step 4: Refer to the GAMMA Table (Table 3). Find that value for R1 closest* to the value for R1 calculated in Step 3, above.

Step 5: Opposite that value for $P(DDLT > R)$ which is closest* to the value for $P(DDLT > R)$ calculated in Step 1 above, read factors F1 and F2 under factor R1 referred to in Step 4, above.

TO CALCULATE THE EXPECTED STOCKOUT DURING LEAD TIME, $E(DDLT > R)$:

$$E(DDLT > R) = F2/L$$
TO CALCULATE THE OPTIMUM REORDER POINT, R:

$$R = F1/L$$

EXAMPLES OF THE USE OF THE NORMAL AND GAMMA TABLES

For the two examples below assume that:
Q = 100.0 hundred lbs.

---

*Or, better, interpolate.

DDLT = 50.4 hundred lbs.
CPU = $11.20 per hundred lbs.
COP = 0.16 per year
DPY = 432.0 hundred lbs.
SC = $3.70 per hundred lbs. short
Example 1: (The NORMAL Table, Table 2)
Assume in this example that:

V = 201.6 hundred lbs. variance during lead time

From the square root table (Table 1) we find $\sqrt{V}$:

$$\sqrt{V} = \sqrt{201.6} = 14.2$$

... and therefore: $\sqrt{V}/DDLT = 14.2/50.4 = .28$

Since the ratio $\sqrt{V}/DDLT$ is less than .5 we should use the NORMAL table (Table 2), and we follow the procedure specified for the NORMAL table:

Step 1:

$$P(DDLT > R) = \frac{11.2 \times .16 \times 100.0}{432.0 \times 3.7 + 11.2 \times .16 \times 100.0} = .11$$

Step 2:   From the NORMAL table we read, opposite
P(DDLT > R) = .11:

F1 = 1.225
F2 = .0524

Therefore: E(DDLT > R) = F2 x $\sqrt{V}$ = .0524 x 14.2 = .744 hundred lbs.

... and: R = DDLT + F1 x $\sqrt{V}$ = 50.4 + 1.225 x 14.2 = 67.8 hundred lbs.

Example 2: (The GAMMA table, Table 3)
Assume in this example that:

V = 10,000 hundred lbs. variance during lead time

From the square root table (Table 1) we find $\sqrt{V}$:

$$\sqrt{V} = \sqrt{10000} = 100.0$$

... and therefore: $\sqrt{V}/DDLT = 100.0/50.4 = 1.98$

Since the ratio $\sqrt{V}/DDLT$ is greater than 0.5 we should use the GAMMA table (Table 3), and we follow the procedure specified for the GAMMA Table:

Step 1:

$$P(DDLT > R) = \frac{11.2 \times .16 \times 1000.0}{432.0 \times 3.7 + 11.2 \times .16 \times 100.0} = .11$$

Step 2: $L = DDLT/V = 50.4/10000$
$= .005$

Step 3: $R1 = DDLT \times L = 50.4 \times .005 = .25$

Step 4: The GAMMA Table closest to $R1 = .25$ is the second GAMMA table, with $R1 = .26$

Step 5: From the GAMMA table identified in Step 4 we read, opposite $P(DDLT > R) = .11$:

$$F1 = .719$$
$$F2 = .072$$

Therefore:
$E(DDLT > R) = F2/L = .072/.005 = 14.4$ hundred lbs.
... and $R = F1/L = .719/.005$
$= 143.7$ hundred lbs.

TABLE 1
—SQUARE ROOTS—

Square roots of numbers other than those given may be found by the following relationships:

$$\sqrt{100n} = 10\sqrt{n}; \quad \sqrt{1000n} = 10\sqrt{10n};$$
$$\sqrt{10000n} = 100\sqrt{n}; \quad \sqrt{(1/10)n} = (1/10)\sqrt{10n};$$
$$\sqrt{(1/100)n} = (1/10)\sqrt{n}; \quad \sqrt{(1/100)n} = (1/100)\sqrt{10n}$$

n	$\sqrt{n}$	n	$\sqrt{n}$	n	$\sqrt{n}$	n	$\sqrt{n}$
1	1.000	51	7.141	101	10.050	151	12.288
2	1.414	52	7.211	102	10.100	152	12.329
3	1.732	53	7.280	103	10.149	153	12.369
4	2.000	54	7.348	104	10.198	154	12.410
5	2.236	55	7.416	105	10.247	155	12.450
6	2.449	56	7.483	106	10.296	156	12.490
7	2.646	57	7.550	107	10.344	157	12.530
8	2.828	58	7.616	108	10.392	158	12.570
9	3.000	59	7.681	109	10.440	159	12.610
10	3.162	60	7.746	110	10.488	160	12.649
11	3.317	61	7.810	111	10.536	161	12.689
12	3.464	62	7.874	112	10.583	162	12.728
13	3.606	63	7.937	113	10.630	163	12.767
14	3.742	64	8.000	114	10.677	164	12.806
15	3.873	65	8.062	115	10.724	165	12.845
16	4.000	66	8.124	116	10.770	166	12.884
17	4.123	67	8.185	117	10.817	167	12.923
18	4.243	68	8.246	118	10.863	168	12.961
19	4.359	69	8.307	119	10.909	169	13.000
20	4.472	70	8.367	120	10.954	170	13.038
21	4.583	71	8.426	121	11.000	171	13.077
22	4.690	72	8.485	122	11.045	172	13.115
23	4.796	73	8.544	123	11.091	173	13.153
24	4.899	74	8.602	124	11.136	174	13.191
25	5.000	75	8.660	125	11.180	175	13.229
26	5.099	76	8.718	126	11.225	176	13.266
27	5.196	77	8.775	127	11.269	177	13.304
28	5.292	78	8.832	128	11.314	178	13.342
29	5.385	79	8.888	129	11.358	179	13.379
30	5.477	80	8.944	130	11.402	180	13.416
31	5.568	81	9.000	131	11.446	181	13.454
32	5.657	82	9.055	132	11.489	182	13.491
33	5.745	83	9.110	133	11.533	183	13.528
34	5.831	84	9.165	134	11.576	184	13.565
35	5.916	85	9.220	135	11.619	185	13.601
36	6.000	86	9.274	136	11.662	186	13.638
37	6.083	87	9.327	137	11.705	187	13.675
38	6.164	88	9.381	138	11.747	188	13.711
39	6.245	89	9.434	139	11.790	189	13.748
40	6.325	90	9.487	140	11.832	190	13.784
41	6.403	91	9.539	141	11.874	191	13.820
42	6.481	92	9.592	142	11.916	192	13.856
43	6.557	93	9.644	143	11.958	193	13.892
44	6.633	94	9.695	144	12.000	194	13.928
45	6.708	95	9.747	145	12.042	195	13.964
46	6.782	96	9.798	146	12.083	196	14.000
47	6.856	97	9.849	147	12.124	197	14.036
48	6.928	98	9.899	148	12.166	198	14.071
49	7.000	99	9.950	149	12.207	199	14.107
50	7.071	100	10.000	150	12.247	200	14.142

(Continued)

MANAGEMENT

TABLE 1 (Continued)
—SQUARE ROOTS—

Square roots of numbers other than those given may be found by the following relationships:

$$\sqrt{100n} = 10\sqrt{n}; \quad \sqrt{1000n} = 10\sqrt{10n};$$
$$\sqrt{10000n} = 100\sqrt{n}; \quad \sqrt{(1/10)n} = (1/10)\sqrt{10n};$$
$$\sqrt{(1/100)n} = (1/10)\sqrt{n}; \quad \sqrt{(1/100)n} = (1/100)\sqrt{10n}$$

n	$\sqrt{n}$	n	$\sqrt{n}$	n	$\sqrt{n}$	n	$\sqrt{n}$
201	14.177	251	15.843	301	17.349	351	18.735
202	14.213	252	15.875	302	17.378	352	18.762
203	14.248	253	15.906	303	17.407	353	18.788
204	14.283	254	15.937	304	17.436	354	18.815
205	14.318	255	15.969	305	17.464	355	18.841
206	14.353	256	16.000	306	17.493	356	18.868
207	14.387	257	16.031	307	17.521	357	18.894
208	14.422	258	16.062	308	17.550	358	18.921
209	14.457	259	16.093	309	17.578	359	18.947
210	14.491	260	16.125	310	17.607	360	18.974
211	14.526	261	16.155	311	17.635	361	19.000
212	14.560	262	16.186	312	17.664	362	19.026
213	14.595	263	16.217	313	17.692	363	19.053
214	14.629	264	16.248	314	17.720	364	19.079
215	14.663	265	16.279	315	17.748	365	19.105
216	14.697	266	16.310	316	17.776	366	19.131
217	14.731	267	16.340	317	17.804	367	19.157
218	14.765	268	16.371	318	17.833	368	19.183
219	14.799	269	16.401	319	17.861	369	19.209
220	14.832	270	16.432	320	17.889	370	19.235
221	14.866	271	16.462	321	17.916	371	19.261
222	14.900	272	16.492	322	17.944	372	19.287
223	14.933	273	16.523	323	17.972	373	19.313
224	14.967	274	16.553	324	18.000	374	19.339
225	15.000	275	16.583	325	18.028	375	19.365
226	15.033	276	16.613	326	18.055	376	19.391
227	15.067	277	16.643	327	18.083	377	19.416
228	15.100	278	16.673	328	18.111	378	19.442
229	15.133	279	16.703	329	18.138	379	19.468
230	15.166	280	16.733	330	18.166	380	19.494
231	15.199	281	16.763	331	18.193	381	19.519
232	15.232	282	16.793	332	18.221	382	19.545
233	15.264	283	16.823	333	18.248	383	19.570
234	15.297	284	16.852	334	18.276	384	19.596
235	15.330	285	16.882	335	18.303	385	19.621
236	15.362	286	16.912	336	18.330	386	19.647
237	15.395	287	16.941	337	18.358	387	19.672
238	15.427	288	16.971	338	18.385	388	19.698
239	15.460	289	17.000	339	18.412	389	19.723
240	15.492	290	17.029	340	18.439	390	19.748
241	15.524	291	17.059	341	18.466	391	19.774
242	15.556	292	17.088	342	18.493	392	19.799
243	15.588	293	17.117	343	18.520	393	19.824
244	15.620	294	17.146	344	18.547	394	19.849
245	15.652	295	17.176	345	18.574	395	19.875
246	15.684	296	17.205	346	18.601	396	19.900
247	15.716	297	17.234	347	18.628	397	19.925
248	15.748	298	17.263	348	18.655	398	19.950
249	15.780	299	17.292	349	18.682	399	19.975
250	15.811	300	17.321	350	18.708	400	20.000

(Continued)

TABLE 1 (Continued)
—SQUARE ROOTS—

Square roots of numbers other than those given may be found
by the following relationships:

$$\sqrt{100n} = 10\sqrt{n}; \quad \sqrt{1000n} = 10\sqrt{10n};$$
$$\sqrt{10000n} = 100\sqrt{n}; \quad \sqrt{(1/10)n} = (1/10)\sqrt{10n};$$
$$\sqrt{(1/100)n} = (1/10)\sqrt{n}; \quad \sqrt{(1/100)n} = (1/100)\sqrt{10n}$$

n	$\sqrt{n}$	n	$\sqrt{n}$	n	$\sqrt{n}$	n	$\sqrt{n}$
401	20.025	451	21.237	501	22.383	551	23.473
402	20.050	452	21.260	502	22.405	552	23.495
403	20.075	453	21.284	503	22.428	553	23.516
404	20.100	454	21.307	504	22.450	554	23.537
405	20.125	455	21.331	505	22.472	555	23.558
406	20.149	456	21.354	506	22.494	556	23.580
407	20.174	457	21.378	507	22.517	557	23.601
408	20.199	458	21.401	508	22.539	558	23.622
409	20.224	459	21.424	509	22.561	559	23.643
410	20.248	460	21.448	510	22.583	560	23.664
411	20.273	461	21.471	511	22.605	561	23.685
412	20.298	462	21.494	512	22.627	562	23.707
413	20.322	463	21.517	513	22.650	563	23.728
414	20.347	464	21.541	514	22.672	564	23.749
415	20.372	465	21.564	515	22.694	565	23.770
416	20.396	466	21.587	516	22.716	566	23.791
417	20.421	467	21.610	517	22.738	567	23.812
418	20.445	468	21.633	518	22.760	568	23.833
419	20.469	469	21.656	519	22.782	569	23.854
420	20.494	470	21.679	520	22.804	570	23.875
421	20.518	471	21.703	521	22.825	571	23.896
422	20.543	472	21.726	522	22.847	572	23.917
423	20.567	473	21.749	523	22.869	573	23.937
424	20.591	474	21.772	524	22.891	574	23.958
425	20.616	475	21.794	525	22.913	575	23.979
426	20.640	476	21.817	526	22.935	576	24.000
427	20.664	477	21.840	527	22.956	577	24.021
428	20.688	478	21.863	528	22.978	578	24.042
429	20.712	479	21.886	529	23.000	579	24.062
430	20.736	480	21.909	530	23.022	580	24.083
431	20.761	481	21.932	531	23.043	581	24.104
432	20.785	482	21.954	532	23.065	582	24.125
433	20.809	483	21.977	533	23.087	583	24.145
434	20.833	484	22.000	534	23.108	584	24.166
435	20.857	485	22.023	535	23.130	585	24.187
436	20.881	486	22.045	536	23.152	586	24.207
437	20.905	487	22.068	537	23.173	587	24.228
438	20.928	488	22.091	538	23.195	588	24.249
439	20.952	489	22.113	539	23.216	589	24.269
440	20.976	490	22.136	540	23.238	590	24.290
441	21.000	491	22.159	541	23.259	591	24.310
442	21.024	492	22.181	542	23.281	592	24.331
443	21.048	493	22.204	543	23.302	593	24.352
444	21.071	494	22.226	544	23.324	594	24.372
445	21.095	495	22.249	545	23.345	595	24.393
446	21.119	496	22.271	546	23.367	596	24.413
447	21.142	497	22.293	547	23.388	597	24.434
448	21.166	498	22.316	548	23.409	598	24.454
449	21.190	499	22.338	549	23.431	599	24.474
450	21.213	500	22.361	550	23.452	600	24.495

(Continued)

TABLE 1 (Continued)
—SQUARE ROOTS—

Square roots of numbers other than those given may be found
by the following relationships:

$$\sqrt{100n} = 10\sqrt{n}; \quad \sqrt{1000n} = 10\sqrt{10n};$$
$$\sqrt{10000n} = 100\sqrt{n}; \quad \sqrt{(1/10)n} = (1/10)\sqrt{10n};$$
$$\sqrt{(1/100)n} = (1/10)\sqrt{n}; \quad \sqrt{(1/100)n} = (1/100)\sqrt{10n}$$

n	$\sqrt{n}$	n	$\sqrt{n}$	n	$\sqrt{n}$	n	$\sqrt{n}$
601	24.515	651	25.515	701	26.476	751	27.404
602	24.536	652	25.534	702	26.495	752	27.423
603	24.556	653	25.554	703	26.514	753	27.441
604	24.576	654	25.573	704	26.533	754	27.459
605	24.597	655	25.593	705	26.552	755	27.477
606	24.617	656	25.612	706	26.571	756	27.495
607	24.637	657	25.632	707	26.589	757	27.514
608	24.658	658	25.652	708	26.608	758	27.532
609	24.678	659	25.671	709	26.627	759	27.550
610	24.698	660	25.690	710	26.646	760	27.568
611	24.718	661	25.710	711	26.665	761	27.586
612	24.739	662	25.729	712	26.683	762	27.604
613	24.759	663	25.749	713	26.702	763	27.622
614	24.779	664	25.768	714	26.721	764	27.641
615	24.799	665	25.788	715	26.739	765	27.659
616	24.819	666	25.807	716	26.758	766	27.677
617	24.839	667	25.826	717	26.777	767	27.695
618	24.860	668	25.846	718	26.796	768	27.713
619	24.880	669	25.865	719	26.814	769	27.731
620	24.900	670	25.884	720	26.833	770	27.749
621	24.920	671	25.904	721	26.851	771	27.767
622	24.940	672	25.923	722	26.870	772	27.785
623	24.960	673	25.942	723	26.889	773	27.803
624	24.980	674	25.962	724	26.907	774	27.821
625	25.000	675	25.981	725	26.926	775	27.839
626	25.020	676	26.000	726	26.944	776	27.857
627	25.040	677	26.019	727	26.963	777	27.875
628	25.060	678	26.038	728	26.981	778	27.893
629	25.080	679	26.058	729	27.000	779	27.911
630	25.100	680	26.077	730	27.019	780	27.928
631	25.120	681	26.096	731	27.037	781	27.946
632	25.140	682	26.115	732	27.055	782	27.964
633	25.159	683	26.134	733	27.074	783	27.982
634	25.179	684	26.153	734	27.092	784	28.000
635	25.199	685	26.173	735	27.111	785	28.018
636	25.219	686	26.192	736	272.19	786	28.036
637	25.239	687	26.211	737	27.148	787	28.054
638	25.259	688	26.230	738	27.166	788	28.071
639	25.278	689	26.249	739	27.185	789	28.089
640	25.298	690	26.268	740	27.203	790	28.107
641	25.318	691	26.287	741	27.221	791	28.125
642	25.338	692	26.306	754	27.240	792	28.142
643	25.357	693	26.325	743	27.258	793	28.160
644	25.377	694	26.344	744	27.276	794	28.178
645	25.397	695	26.363	745	27.295	795	28.196
646	25.417	696	26.382	746	27.313	796	28.213
647	25.436	697	26.401	747	27.331	797	28.231
648	25.456	698	26.420	748	27.350	798	28.249
649	25.475	699	26.439	749	27.368	799	28.267
650	25.495	700	26.458	750	27.386	800	28.284

(Continued)

TABLE 1 (Continued)
—SQUARE ROOTS—

Square roots of numbers other than those given may be found
by the following relationships:

$$\sqrt{100n} = 10\sqrt{n}; \quad \sqrt{1000n} = 10\sqrt{10n};$$
$$\sqrt{10000n} = 100\sqrt{n}; \quad \sqrt{(1/10)n} = (1/10)\sqrt{10n};$$
$$\sqrt{(1/100)n} = (1/10)\sqrt{n}; \quad \sqrt{(1/100)n} = (1/100)\sqrt{10n}$$

n	$\sqrt{n}$	n	$\sqrt{n}$	n	$\sqrt{n}$	n	$\sqrt{n}$
801	28.302	851	29.172	901	30.017	951	30.838
802	28.320	852	29.189	902	30.033	952	30.854
803	28.337	853	29.206	903	30.050	953	30.871
804	28.355	854	29.223	904	30.067	954	30.887
805	28.373	855	29.240	905	30.083	955	30.903
806	28.390	856	29.257	906	30.100	956	30.919
807	28.408	857	29.275	907	30.116	957	30.935
808	28.425	858	29.292	908	30.133	958	30.952
809	28.443	859	29.309	909	30.150	959	30.968
810	28.460	860	29.326	910	30.166	960	30.984
811	28.478	861	29.343	911	30.183	961	31.000
812	28.496	862	29.360	912	30.199	962	31.016
813	28.513	863	29.377	913	30.216	963	31.032
814	28.531	864	29.394	914	30.232	964	31.048
815	28.548	865	29.411	915	30.249	965	31.064
816	28.566	866	29.428	916	30.265	966	31.081
817	28.583	867	29.445	917	30.282	967	31.097
818	28.601	868	29.462	918	30.299	968	31.113
819	28.618	869	29.479	919	30.315	969	31.129
820	28.636	870	29.496	920	30.332	970	31.145
821	28.653	871	29.513	921	30.348	971	31.161
822	28.671	872	29.530	922	30.364	972	31.177
823	28.688	873	29.547	923	30.381	973	31.193
824	28.705	874	29.563	924	30.397	974	31.209
825	28.723	875	29.580	925	30.414	975	31.225
826	28.740	876	29.597	926	30.430	976	31.241
827	28.758	877	29.614	927	30.447	977	31.257
828	28.775	878	29.631	928	30.463	978	31.273
829	28.792	879	29.648	929	30.480	979	31.289
830	28.810	880	29.665	930	30.496	980	31.305
831	28.827	881	29.682	931	30.512	981	31.321
832	28.844	882	29.698	932	30.529	982	31.337
833	28.862	883	29.715	933	30.545	983	31.353
834	28.879	884	29.732	934	30.561	984	31.369
835	28.896	885	29.749	935	30.578	985	31.385
836	28.914	886	29.766	936	30.594	986	31.401
837	28.931	887	29.783	937	30.610	987	31.417
838	28.948	888	29.799	938	30.627	988	31.432
839	28.965	889	29.816	939	30.643	989	31.448
840	28.983	890	29.833	940	30.659	990	31.464
841	29.000	891	29.850	941	30.676	991	31.480
842	29.017	892	29.866	942	30.692	992	31.496
843	29.034	893	29.883	943	30.708	993	31.512
844	29.052	894	29.900	944	30.725	994	31.528
845	29.069	895	29.917	945	30.741	995	31.544
846	29.086	896	29.933	946	30.757	996	31.559
847	29.103	897	29.950	947	30.773	997	31.575
848	29.120	898	29.967	948	30.790	998	31.591
849	29.138	899	29.983	949	30.806	999	31.607
850	29.155	900	30.000	950	30.822	1000	31.623

(Continued)

MANAGEMENT

TABLE 2

—NORMAL—

P(DDLT>R)	F1	F2	P(DDLT>R)	F1	F2
.500	.000	.4030	.115	1.200	.0553
.490	.025	.3905	.110	1.225	.0524
.480	.050	.3782	.106	1.250	.0497
.470	.075	.3662	.101	1.275	.0470
.460	.100	.3544	.097	1.300	.0445
5.40	.125	.3429	.093	1.325	.0421
.440	.150	.3317	.089	1.350	.0398
.431	.175	.3207	.085	1.375	.0375
.421	.200	.3099	.081	1.400	.0354
.411	.225	.2994	.077	1.425	.0334
.401	.250	.2891	.074	1.450	.0315
.392	.275	.2791	.070	1.475	.0296
.382	.300	.2693	.067	1.500	.0279
.373	.325	.2597	.064	1.525	.0262
.363	.350	.2504	.061	1.550	.0246
.354	.375	.2413	.058	1.575	.0231
.345	.400	.2325	.055	1.600	.0217
.335	.425	.2239	.052	1.625	.0203
.326	.450	.2155	.049	1.650	.0190
.317	.475	.2073	.047	1.675	.0178
.309	.500	.1994	.045	1.700	.0166
.300	.525	.1917	.042	1.725	.0155
.291	.550	.1842	.040	1.750	.0144
.283	.575	.1769	.038	1.775	.0134
.274	.600	.1699	.036	1.800	.0125
.266	.625	.1630	.034	1.825	.0116
.258	.650	.1564	.032	1.850	.0107
.250	.675	.1499	.030	1.875	.0099
.242	.700	.1437	.029	1.900	.0092
.234	.725	.1376	.027	1.925	.0084
.227	.750	.1318	.026	1.950	.0078
.219	.775	.1261	.024	1.975	.0071
.212	.800	.1206	.023	2.000	.0065
.205	.825	.1153	.021	2.025	.0060
.198	.850	.1102	.020	2.050	.0054
.191	.875	.1053	.019	2.075	.0049
.184	.900	.1005	.018	2.100	.0044
.177	.925	.0959	.017	2.125	.0040
.171	.950	.0914	.016	2.150	.0036
.165	.975	.0872	.015	2.175	.0032
.159	1.000	.0831	.014	2.200	.0028
.153	1.025	.0791	.013	2.225	.0025
.147	1.050	.0753	.012	2.250	.0021
.141	1.075	.0716	.011	2.275	.0018
.136	1.100	.0681	.011	2.300	.0015
.130	1.125	.0647	.010	2.325	.0013
.125	1.150	.0614	.009	2.350	.0010
.120	1.175	.0583	.009	2.375	.0008

TABLE 3

—GAMMA—

| R1 = | .20 | | .26 | | .34 | | .44 | |
P(DDLT>R)	F1	F2	F1	F2	F1	F2	F1	F2
.010	2.205	.002	2.477	.002	2.796	.002	3.133	.002
.020	1.675	.010	1.927	.010	2.216	.011	2.533	.011
.030	1.381	.017	1.617	.018	1.890	.019	2.192	.020
.040	1.181	.024	1.404	.025	1.665	.027	1.952	.028
.050	1.031	.031	1.244	.033	1.493	.035	1.769	.037
.060	.913	.037	1.116	.040	1.356	.042	1.622	.045
.070	.816	.043	1.011	.046	1.242	.050	1.499	.053
.080	.735	.050	.922	.053	1.144	.057	1.394	.060
.090	.665	.056	.845	.060	1.060	.064	1.303	.068
.100	.605	.061	.778	.066	.986	.071	1.222	.076
.110	.552	.067	.719	.072	.920	.078	1.149	.084
.120	.506	.072	.666	.078	.861	.085	1.084	.091
.130	.464	.077	.618	.084	.808	.091	1.024	.099
.140	.426	.082	.575	.090	.759	.098	.970	.106
.150	.392	.087	.536	.096	.714	.105	.920	.113
.160	.362	.092	.500	.101	.673	.111	.873	.120
.170	.334	.097	.467	.107	.635	.117	.830	.127
.180	.308	.101	.437	.112	.599	.123	.790	.134
.190	.285	.105	.409	.117	.566	.130	.752	.141
.200	.264	.110	.383	.122	.536	.135	.717	.148
.210	.244	.114	.359	.127	.507	.141	.684	.155
.220	.226	.118	.336	.132	.480	.147	.652	.162
.230	.209	.121	.315	.137	.455	.153	.623	.169
.240	.193	.125	.296	.141	.431	.158	.595	.175
.250	.179	.129	.277	.146	.408	.164	.568	.182
.260	.166	.132	.260	.150	.387	.169	.543	.188
.270	.153	.135	.244	.155	.367	.175	.519	.194
.280	.142	.138	.229	.159	.348	.180	.496	.201
.290	.131	.141	.215	.163	.330	.185	.474	.207
.300	.121	.144	.201	.167	.313	.190	.454	.213
.310	.112	.147	.189	.171	.297	.195	.434	.219
.320	.103	.150	.177	.174	.281	.200	.415	.225
.330	.095	.153	.166	.178	.266	.205	.396	.231
.340	.088	.155	.155	.182	.252	.209	.379	.237
.350	.081	.157	.145	.185	.239	.214	.362	.243
.360	.074	.160	.136	.188	.227	.218	.346	.248
.370	.069	.162	.127	.191	.214	.223	.331	.254
.380	.063	.164	.118	.195	.203	.227	.316	.259
.390	.058	.166	.111	198	.192	.231	.302	.265
.400	.053	.168	.103	.201	.182	.236	.288	.270
.410	.049	.170	.096	.203	.172	.240	.275	.276
.420	.044	.171	.090	.206	.162	.244	.262	.281
.430	.041	.173	.083	.209	.153	.247	.250	.286
.440	.037	.174	.078	.211	.144	.251	.239	.291
.450	.034	.176	.072	.214	.136	.255	.227	.296
.460	.031	.177	.067	.216	.128	.258	.217	.301
.470	.028	.179	.062	.218	.121	.262	.206	.306
.480	.025	.180	.057	.221	.114	.265	.196	.311
.490	.023	.181	.053	.223	.107	.269	.186	.315
.500	.021	.182	.049	.225	.100	.272	.177	.320

(Continued)

TABLE 3 (Continued)

—GAMMA—

P(DDLT>R)	.57 F1	F2	.74 F1	F2	.96 F1	F2	1.25 F1	F2
.010	3.527	.003	3.987	.003	4.516	.003	5.165	.004
.202	2.898	.012	3.327	.013	3.826	.014	4.435	.015
.030	2.537	.021	2.947	.022	3.424	.024	4.005	.026
.040	2.285	.030	2.677	.032	3.139	.034	3.701	.036
.050	2.090	.039	2.471	.041	2.918	.044	3.465	.047
.060	1.933	.047	2.301	.050	2.738	.054	3.271	.058
.070	1.801	.056	2.160	.060	2.585	.064	3.106	.068
.080	1.688	.064	2.037	.069	2.454	.073	2.964	.079
.090	1.589	.073	1.930	.078	2.337	.083	2.838	.090
.100	1.500	.081	1.834	.087	2.233	.093	2.724	.100
.110	1.420	.090	1.748	.096	2.139	.103	2.622	.111
.120	1.349	.098	1.669	.105	2.053	.113	2.528	.122
.130	1.283	.106	1.597	.114	1.974	.123	2.441	.133
.140	1.223	.114	1.531	.123	1.901	.133	2.361	.144
.150	1.167	.122	1.469	.132	1.833	.143	2.286	.155
.160	1.115	.130	1.411	.141	1.770	.152	2.216	.165
.170	1.067	.138	1.357	.150	1.710	.162	2.150	.176
.180	1.022	.146	1.307	.159	1.654	.172	2.087	.187
.190	.980	.154	1.259	.167	1.601	.182	2.028	.198
.200	9.40	.162	1.214	.176	1.551	.192	1.972	.209
.210	.902	.170	1.171	.185	1.503	.202	1.918	.220
.220	.866	.177	1.131	.194	1.457	.211	1.866	.231
.230	.832	.185	1.092	.203	1.413	.221	1.817	.242
.240	.800	.192	1.055	.211	1.371	.231	1.770	.253
.250	.769	.200	1.020	.220	1.331	.241	1.725	.264
.260	.739	.208	.986	.228	1.293	.251	1.681	.276
.270	.711	.215	.954	.237	1.256	.260	1.639	.287
.280	.684	.222	.922	.246	1.220	.270	1.599	.298
.290	.658	.230	.892	.254	1.186	.280	1.560	.309
.300	.634	.237	.864	.263	1.152	.290	1.522	.309
.310	.610	.244	.836	.271	1.120	.300	1.485	.331
.320	.587	.251	.809	.280	1.089	.309	1.449	.343
.330	.565	.259	.783	.288	1.059	.319	1.414	.354
.340	.544	.266	.758	.296	1.030	.329	1.381	.365
.350	.524	.273	.734	.305	1.002	.339	1.348	.377
.360	.504	.280	.711	.313	.974	.348	1.316	.388
.370	.485	.287	.688	.321	.947	.358	1.285	.399
.380	.467	.293	.666	.330	.921	.368	1.254	.411
.390	.449	.300	.644	.338	.896	.378	1.225	.422
.400	.432	.307	.624	.346	.871	.388	1.196	.434
.410	.416	.314	.604	.354	.847	.397	1.167	.445
.420	.400	.320	.584	.362	.824	.407	1.140	.457
.430	.384	.327	.565	.370	.801	.417	1.113	.468
.440	.369	.333	.546	.378	.779	.426	1.086	.480
.450	.355	.340	.528	.386	.757	.436	1.060	.491
.460	.341	.346	.511	.394	.736	.446	1.035	.503
.470	.327	.353	.494	.402	.715	.456	1.009	.514
.480	.314	.359	.477	.410	.694	.465	.985	.526
.490	.301	.365	.461	.418	.674	.475	.961	.538
.500	.289	.371	.445	.426	.655	.485	.937	.550

(Continued)

TABLE 3 (Continued)

—GAMMA—

R1 = P(DDLT>R)	1.63 F1	F2	2.12 F1	F2	2.76 F1	F2	3.57 F1	F2
.010	5.934	.004	6.865	.005	8.006	.006	9.362	.007
.020	5.164	.016	6.045	.017	7.126	.019	8.422	.021
.030	4.710	.027	5.562	.030	6.606	.032	7.862	.035
.040	4.385	.039	5.212	.042	6.230	.045	7.456	.049
.050	4.132	.050	4.938	.054	5.935	.059	7.136	.064
.060	3.922	.062	4.713	.066	5.691	.072	6.871	.078
.070	3.744	.073	4.520	.079	5.481	.086	6.643	.093
.080	3.590	.085	4.353	.092	5.298	.099	6.445	.108
.090	3.452	.097	4.203	.104	5.135	.113	6.265	.123
.100	3.329	.108	4.068	.117	4.988	.127	6.104	.139
.110	3.217	.120	3.946	.130	4.853	.141	5.957	.154
.120	3.114	.132	3.833	.143	4.729	.156	5.821	.170
.130	3.019	.144	3.728	.156	4.614	.170	5.694	.186
.140	2.931	.156	3.631	.169	4.507	.185	5.576	.201
.150	2.848	.168	3.540	.182	4.406	.199	5.465	.218
.160	2.770	.180	3.454	.196	4.311	.214	5.360	.234
.170	2.697	.192	3.373	.209	4.222	.229	5.260	.250
.180	2.628	.204	3.296	.223	4.136	.244	5.166	.267
.190	2.562	.216	3.223	.236	4.055	.259	5.075	.284
.200	2.499	.228	3.153	.250	3.977	.274	4.989	.300
.210	2.439	.241	3.086	.263	3.902	.289	4.906	.317
.220	2.381	.253	3.022	.277	3,830	.305	4.826	.335
.230	2.326	.265	2.960	.291	3.761	.320	4.749	.352
.240	2.273	.278	2.900	.305	3.694	.336	4.674	.370
.250	2.222	.290	2.843	.319	3.630	.352	4.602	.387
.260	2.173	.303	2.788	.333	3.568	.367	4.533	.405
.270	2.126	.315	2.734	.347	3.508	.383	4.465	.423
.280	2.080	.328	2.682	.362	3.449	.399	4.399	.441
.290	2.035	.341	2.632	.376	3.392	.416	4.334	.459
.300	1.992	.353	2.583	.390	3.337	.432	4.272	.478
.310	1.950	.366	2.535	.405	3.283	.448	4.211	.496
.320	1.909	.379	2.488	.420	3.230	.465	4.152	.515
.330	1.870	.392	2.443	.434	3.178	.482	4.094	.534
.340	1.831	.405	2.399	.449	3.128	.499	4.037	.553
.350	1.793	.418	2.356	.464	3.079	.516	3.981	.572
.360	1.756	.431	2.314	.479	3.031	.533	3.926	.592
.370	1.720	.444	2.272	.494	2.983	.550	3.872	.611
.380	1.685	.458	2.232	.509	2.937	.567	3.819	.631
.390	1.650	.471	2.192	.525	2.892	.585	3.767	.651
.400	1.617	.484	2.153	.540	2.847	.603	3.176	.671
.410	1.583	.498	2.115	.555	2803	.620	3.666	.692
.420	1.551	.511	2.078	.571	2.760	.638	3.617	.712
.430	1.519	.525	2.041	.587	2.717	.656	3.568	.733
.440	1.488	.538	2.005	.602	2.675	.675	3.520	.754
.450	1.457	.552	1.969	.618	2.634	.693	3.472	.775
.460	1.427	.565	1.934	.634	2.593	.712	3.425	.796
.470	1.398	.579	1.899	.651	2.553	.730	3.379	.818
.480	1.368	.593	1.865	.667	2.513	.749	3.333	.840
.490	1.340	.607	1.831	.683	2.474	.768	3.288	.862
.500	1.312	.621	1.798	.700	2.435	.788	3.243	.884